CHISWICK
PAST

First published 1995
by Historical Publications Ltd
32 Ellington Street, London N7 8PL
(Tel: 0171-607 1628)

ISBN 0 948667 33 8
British Library Cataloguing-in-Publication Data
A catalogue record for this book is available from the British Library.

Typeset in Palatino by Historical Publications Ltd
Reproduction by G & J Graphics, London EC1
Printed in Zaragoza, Spain by Edelvives.

CHISWICK PAST

Gillian Clegg

HISTORICAL PUBLICATIONS

Acknowledgements

The author would particularly like to thank Chiswick Local Studies Librarian, Carolyn Hammond, for her invaluable help. She would also like to thank Val Bott, Jonathan Cotton, Tom Greeves, Carolyn and Peter Hammond, Bob Troop and James Wisdom for reading and commenting on draft chapters, and Andrea Cameron, Lawrence Duttson, Tony Lewis, June Lewing, Alan Martin and Shirley Seaton for their assistance.

The Illustrations

The author and publisher would like to thank the following organisations and individuals for allowing their pictures to be reproduced in this book, especially the Leisure Services Department of the London Borough of Hounslow for their kind permission to reproduce a large number of illustrations from the Chiswick Local Studies Collection and Gunnersbury Park Museum.

Brentford and Chiswick Times *150*
Chiswick Local Studies Collection *2, 6, 7, 8, 10, 11, 13, 14, 15, 17, 18, 21, 22, 23, 24, 25, 26, 27, 28, 29, 30, 31, 32, 33, 36, 37, 39, 41, 42, 43, 44, 45, 46, 47, 48, 50, 51, 53, 55, 56, 58, 59, 60, 61, 63, 65, 66, 67, 69, 70, 71, 74, 75, 76, 77, 78, 79, 82, 83, 84, 85, 86, 87, 88??, 89, 90, 91, 92, 93, 94, 96, 97, 98, 99, 102, 107, 109, 111, 112, 115, 116, 117, 119, 120, 121, 122, 123, 124, 125, 127, 128, 130??, 131, 132, 134, 135, 136, 137, 138, 139, 140, 141, 142, 148, 149, 152, 153, 155, 156, 157, 158, 160, 162, 164, 165, 166, 167, 168, 170, 171, 173, 175, 176, 177, 178.*
Gillian Clegg *145*
Peter Downes *19, 172*
Fuller's Brewery *103*
John Gillham *88, 118*
T.A .Greeves *62, 80, 113, 147, 159*
Gunnersbury Park Museum *cover illustration, 101, 104, 108, 143, 169, 174*
Huntington Art Gallery and Museum *72*
London Borough of Hounslow Local Studies *68*
London Borough of Richmond *20*
Alan Martin *9, 12, 16, 34, 49, 95, 100, 110, 129, 146, 151, 163*
Museum of London *4, 35*
J.C. Newton *161*
Tom Parker *40*
Jane Perkins *130*
St Michael and All Angels church, Bedford Park *154*
Shirley Seaton *1*
Victoria County History *73*
Vosper Thornycroft *105, 106*
West London Archaeological Field Group *3, 5*

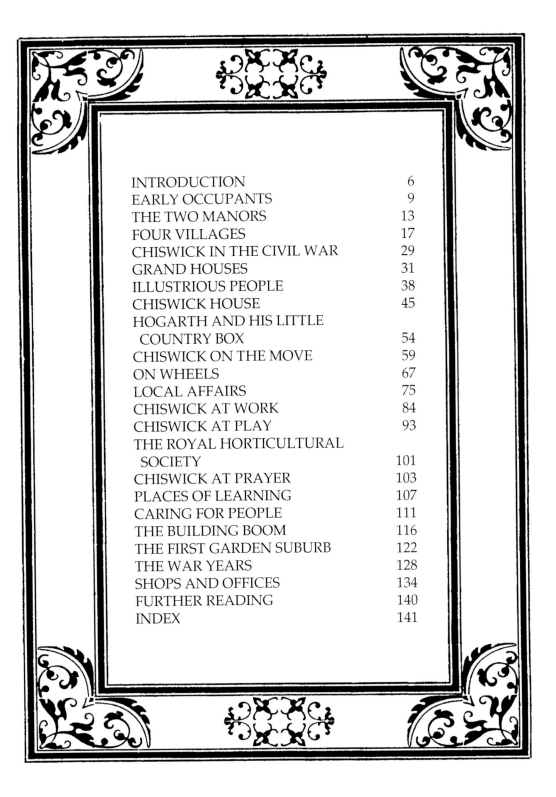

Introduction

Chiswick, with its pretty riverside villages and position on the main route to the west of England, was a popular country retreat for City dwellers from the sixteenth century onwards. Painter William Hogarth, writer Alexander Pope, and poet W.B.Yeats, were among many famous residents. A large number of Chiswick's handsome early buildings still survive, including Chiswick House, the important Palladian-style villa designed by the 3rd Earl of Burlington.

Chiswick was also the scene of a decisive skirmish in the Civil War; the home of the Royal Horticultural Society's early experimental gardens; the location of the first 'garden suburb' and where, in World War II, the first V2 rocket landed.

Perhaps surprisingly, Chiswick also boasts some notable industrial achievements: the first naval torpedo boats were built in Chiswick, and products such as Cherry Blossom boot polish and linoleum were invented there.

'Chiswick' is a Saxon name meaning 'farm where cheese was made' (Keswick in Cumbria means exactly the same). In earlier centuries, Chiswick was just the name of one of four small villages lying in a large loop of the River Thames (Little Sutton, Turnham Green and Strand-on-the-Green were the others). By the nineteenth century, Chiswick parish embraced all these villages. However, the name, Chiswick, apart from being used in voting wards, no longer has any meaning for administrative or political purposes: in 1965 the Borough of Brentford and Chiswick was absorbed into the Borough of Hounslow, and, in 1974, Chiswick was phased out of the parliamentary constituency name.

The boundary of the old parish of Chiswick with the adjoining parishes of Acton, Brentford and Hammersmith is shown on the map on page 63. This book, however, has taken a slight liberty in extending the area defined as Chiswick slightly north, to follow the line of the W4 postal area, some of which lies in the old parish of Acton, now administered by the Borough of Ealing. The W4 postal area is bounded on the west by the railway line that runs from Kew Bridge to Acton Central; on the north by the public playing fields in Southfield Road, and to the east by Hatfield Road, Greenend Road and the west side of Emlyn road. Here it meets the northern boundary of the Borough of Hounslow and links with the old Chiswick/Hammersmith boundary at the junction with Stamford Brook Road.

Chiswick is practically enclosed by the large meander made by the River Thames. Most of the area is about 6m above sea level, rising in the north-west corner. Flood plain gravels cover nearly all the Chiswick peninsula and brickearths most of the northern area. Being generally low lying, Chiswick was quite watery: early maps are dotted with ponds and lakes and several streams (now underground) ran through the area. The Bollo Brook, rising on Hanger Hill ran down Bollo Lane, west of Turnham Green to the grounds of Chiswick House. There it was canalised to form the lake, but is now under the lake in a conduit, flowing into the river at the end of the Promenade Approach Road: this stream sometimes flooded Acton Green.

Several branches of the Stamford Brook from Acton also flowed through the area. One branch ran down Horn Lane across Acton High Street, north of the public playing fields in Southfield Road, along the eastern edge of Bedford Park to Stamford Brook. Another branch, rising in Mill Hill (this stream is sometimes called the Mill Hill Brook) took a winding course, roughly on the line of Acton Lane before turning sharply eastwards across Acton Green and along the line of the Bath Road. These two streams converged with another branch of the Stamford Brook at Ravenscourt Park and flowed into the Thames at the Creek, Hammersmith.

A tributary of the Mill Hill Brook possibly formed the Hammersmith/Chiswick boundary running south along the line of Goldhawk Road/British Grove and flowing into the river where there is now a humpbacked bridge at the eastern end of Chiswick Mall. Another stream, probably rising at Spring Grove, ran west-east across Chiswick, probably joining the Bollo Brook before it entered the grounds of Chiswick House.

Today, despite the fact that traffic snarls up Chiswick High Road and thunders down the A4, Chiswick still retains a great deal of its charm and its history. It contains five designated conservation areas and many of its older buildings are listed by English Heritage.

Taking different themes, this book traces the history and development of Chiswick from prehistoric times to the present day.

1. Young's Corner where Chiswick begins. It marks the boundary of the old parishes of Chiswick and Hammersmith and was also the dividing line of the old County of Middlesex from the County of London. The corner gets its name from a grocer's shop on the site run by a family called Young. The name is preserved on this plaque on the Victorian building put up in 1894.

2. *A view of the River Thames from Chiswick, by Charles White in the eighteenth century. As this picture illustrates, the Thames was a much wider and shallower river before the banks were built up.*

Early Occupants

How long have people lived in Chiswick? The archaeological evidence suggests they may have been here since the Ice Age.

The first people to live in Britain arrived about half a million years ago during one of the warmer spells of the Ice Age, probably coming across the land bridge which linked Britain to the European continent. They were nomadic, following the herds of animals they relied on for their food. All they left behind were the flint tools they used, the most common being the all-purpose hand axe, used for chopping and cutting meat, sinew and bone. These hand axes have been found in Chiswick: in Stile Hall Parade, at Turnham Green, Chiswick Park and in Duke's Meadows.

The Ice Age ended around 8,500 BC and Britain became separated from the Continent between six and seven thousand years ago as the melting glaciers caused the rivers and seas to rise. The climate now became warmer and wetter and different tools were needed. An axe dating to this period was discovered in Hartington Road.

As people gradually learnt how to cultivate crops and to herd animals they were able to swap the nomadic existence for a more settled lifestyle around 4,500 BC. Flint tools and pottery of this date have been found on Chiswick Eyot, suggesting an early settlement there. Corney Reach and Strand-on-the-Green have also produced flint tools.

The discovery of how to make more effective tools out of metal arrived in Britain about the middle of the third millennium BC. The first metal to be used was copper, then bronze, followed by iron. An early bronze rapier was found at Homefield Recreation Ground and traces of occupation in the later Bronze Age (during the 9th-8th centuries BC) were found on the site of the old London Transport bus depot opposite Gunnersbury station. Archaeologists found holes that once contained posts, the wood long rotted away, together with a large quantity of pottery.

It is rare to find axes made of bronze still in their wooden hafts but an axe in its handle was found when the third Kew Bridge was being constructed. It was presented to Edward VII at the bridge opening ceremony in 1903. It then disappeared for many years before surfacing again at an auction in 1994 when it was bought by the Museum of London.

HUMAN SKULLS IN THE RIVER

Systematic dredging of the river Thames in the last century revealed many archaeological finds and, more curiously, a large number of human skulls. According to a report in the *Archaeological Journal* 1929, over a hundred of these came from the river opposite Strand-on-the-Green. These have disappeared (prob-

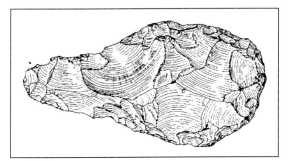

3. *The all-purpose handaxe used by early British inhabitants. Examples have been found in Chiswick.*

4. *This bronze axe, still in its wooden socket, was found at Kew Bridge and is now in the Museum of London.*

ably carried off by collectors), but radiocarbon dating of river skulls found elsewhere suggests they belonged to people living around 600 BC (the end of the Bronze Age and beginning of the Iron Age).

Since most of the skulls analysed were males aged between 25 and 35, it is tempting to think they were the victims of some bloody battle, but river burial could have been a common practice then, very few burials of this date have been found on land in Britain and it is known that weapons were deposited in rivers as offerings to the gods – perhaps skulls too..

THE ROMANS IN CHISWICK

The main Roman road to the west of England runs through Chiswick. It is thought to start at Newgate Street in the City and follow the line of Holborn Viaduct, Oxford Street, Bayswater Road, Goldhawk Road, Bath Road, Acton Green, Chiswick High Road, then on to Kew Bridge Road, Brentford High Street to the important Roman towns of *Pontes* (Staines), *Calleva Atrebatum* (Silchester) and the west.

Somewhere around Turnham Green this road probably converged with another, less important, Roman road known as Akeman Street in Saxon times which is thought to run from Ludgate Circus along Fleet Street, Kensington High Street, Hammersmith Road, King Street and Chiswick High Road (although it might have lain further south, along the course of Wellesley Road, before the two roads merged).

Traces of these Roman roads have never been revealed in archaeological excavations in Chiswick so their exact course is uncertain. However, the more northerly road almost certainly marked the Acton/Chiswick boundary until 1894 when the boundary was adjusted slightly south to follow the railway line.

It is likely that the northern Roman road and/or its ditches were still visible when the boundary was defined, probably somewhere around the ninth or tenth centuries. William Stukeley, an antiquary, attempting to follow the line of this road in 1722, says 'between Staines and London it is the common road till you come to Turnham Green: there the present

road through Hammersmith and Kensington leaves it; for it passes more northward upon the common where to a discerning eye the trace of it is manifest'.

This road had obviously gone out of use in the eighteenth century since Stukeley comments further: 'I rode the broken part of it between Acton Road and Turnham Green. It is still a narrow, straight way, keeping its original direction, but full of dangerous sloughs, being a clayey soil and never repaired.'

A few sherds of Roman pottery (now in Gunnersbury Park Museum) have been found in the gardens of Bedford House on South Parade – which might lie along the line of the road – and an urn of silver Roman coins (now lost) was found in 1781 at Turnham Green.

People lived down by the river in Roman times. A pit containing Roman building material and Roman rubbish was found under the Regency Quay development in Pumping Station Road, flue tiles and a piece of mortaria – a vessel used for grinding corn – on Chiswick Mall, and pottery on Chiswick Eyot, Strand-on-the-Green and Duke's Meadows.

SAXON WARRIORS

The Saxons had to fight to establish themselves in England and several centuries later they had to resist Viking invaders. The *Anglo Saxon Chronicles* tell us that twice in the year 1016 King Edmund of England pursued the Danes led by Canute across the Thames at Brentford.

It is perhaps not surprising that all Saxon finds from Chiswick so far are of a military nature – spearheads, the remains of a shield and knives from in and around the river. The decorated pommel of a Saxon sword and scraps of armour were found at Strand on the Green.

5. *Archaeologists in Brentford High Street, excavating the Roman road that ran through Chiswick and Brentford.*

6. *These Roman and Saxon finds from West London were made by antiquarians in the 19th century. The Roman pottery vessels, Nos. 13, 15 and 16 were found in or near the Thames at Chiswick; as were the Saxon spearhead (No. 17) and the shield boss (19).*

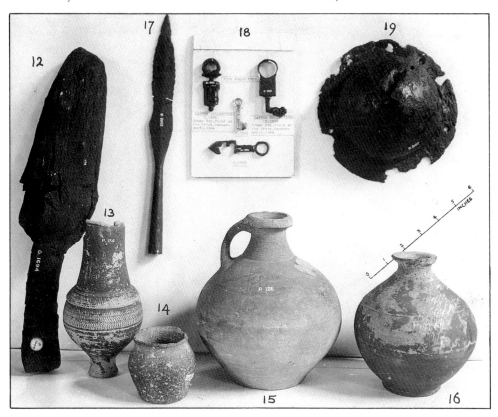

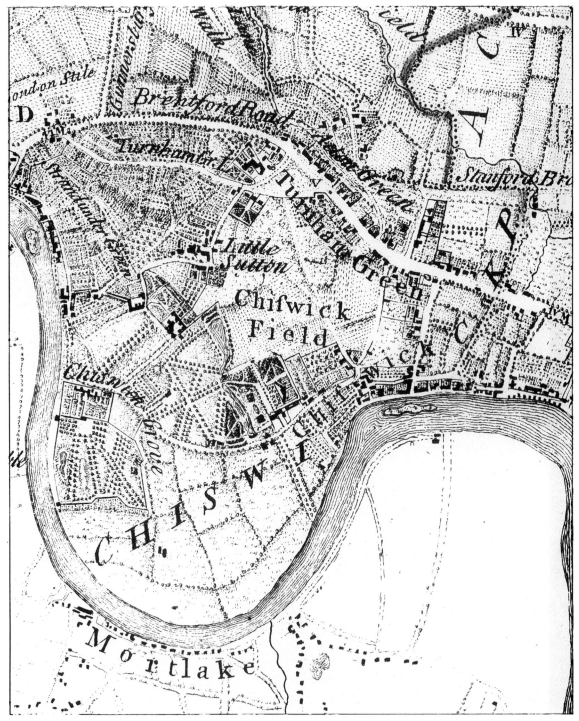

7. *John Rocque's map of c.1745, showing the roads and villages in Chiswick. The area didn't change much until the later nineteenth century.*

The Two Manors

Chiswick isn't mentioned in the Domesday Book (the record of landholdings compiled for William the Conqueror in 1086) since it was already part of the large estate of Fulham, owned by the Dean and Chapter of the Cathedral church of St Paul.

By the twelfth century, St Paul's owned two manors in Chiswick: Sutton Manor, containing three hides, and Chiswick Prebendal Manor, two hides (the area of hides varied but was frequently around 120 acres).

SUTTON MANOR

Sutton Manor was first recorded in 1181 (Sutton means 'south farm'). It contained 330 acres of arable land, 16 acres of meadow and about 13 acres of woodland. The manor, which had a watermill by 1458, was probably always leased out; in the fourteenth and fifteenth centuries it was held by the Crown.

King Richard II built a residence in Sutton in 1396. Records show that £928. 12s. 3d was spent on it, using timbers from the temporary parliament building in Westminster. The house stood within a moat and consisted of a hall, a chapel, two chambers with two solars above and a cellar beneath. A medieval undercroft almost certainly belonging to this house came to light in 1905 – at the time it was thought to be a Roman vault.

Henry IV used this house. So did Henry V, but he doesn't appear to have liked it since he gave orders for it to be pulled down in 1415. However, a new house must have been erected shortly after as Henry VI issued state papers from Chiswick between 1441 and 1443.

The manor house stood on the corner of what is now Fauconberg Road and Sutton Court Road. It was referred to as Sutton 'Beauregard' in the 1430s, presumably because of its pleasant view across the river to the Surrey Hills, and known as Sutton Court by c.1537.

Later lessees of Sutton manor were, among others, Sir Thomas More in 1524; Chaloner Chute, speaker of

9. Ice House, Grove Park Road. Workmen came across the remains of this in 1949. It probably stood in the grounds of Sutton Court. Used for storing ice and perhaps for keeping vegetables out of season, it was originally a hollow brick dome covering a circular underground chamber, insulated with a thick layer of puddled clay.

8. Sutton Court in 1844. The old manor house had been largely rebuilt by 1795.

10. *Chiswick from the river, engraved for Harrison's* History of London *c.1775. The buildings on the right include the Prebendal manor house and other buildings used by Westminster School in times of plague.*

the House of Commons in 1639; and Viscount Fauconberg in 1675. Lord Burlington began to acquire land from Sutton Manor in the 1720s and, in 1800, St Paul's sold the remainder (but not the manorial rights) to the Duke of Devonshire.

The mansion which stood at Sutton in 1589 had a gatehouse, malthouse and farm buildings, including a dovecote, set within orchards and gardens of three acres. In 1674 the house was described as 'fit to receive a family of 40 or 50' when it had twelve acres of walled garden. In 1691 it possessed a maze and a bowling green. The house was largely rebuilt in 1795, became a boy's school in 1845 before being demolished at the end of the nineteenth century. In 1905 the block of flats called Sutton Court was put up on the site.

CHISWICK MANOR

Chiswick Manor was known as the Prebendal Manor since revenue from the estate was used to support the prebendary member for Chiswick of the chapter of St Paul's. A famous Chiswick prebend was preacher and poet, Dr John Donne, in 1622.

The manor house stood on Chiswick Mall, to the east of Chiswick Lane South. In the sixteenth century, the then Prebend of Chiswick, Gabriel Goodman, who was also the Dean of Westminster, decided to use the property as a retreat in times of sickness for pupils of Westminster Collegiate School, and in 1570 the whole estate was leased to Westminster which promptly subleased the property it didn't want and kept what it did: ie the manor house.

In order to accommodate the prebendary, the master and usher of Westminster School and forty children, the manor house was extended by a new building erected on the west side. Known as College House by 1649, it stood on the east corner of Chiswick Lane South. By 1706 the manor house was 'ruinous' and was replaced by a substantial brick house.

In 1810 College House became a girls' boarding school and in 1818 home to the Chiswick Press until 1852. After that it was leased and used as a lecture hall until 1875 when it was pulled down and 'decently buried beneath some modern villas' – The Hollies, Suffolk House, Staithe House.

12. Chiswick and Hammersmith parish boundary stones at the bottom of Stamford Brook Avenue (near the petrol station). Before the boundary was adjusted in 1994, it went right through a house in Emlyn Road! No. 69 paid one third of its rates to Hounslow and two thirds to Hammersmith.

11. College House (on the left) and the brick house that replaced the old Chiswick manor house on Chiswick Mall (the corner with Chiswick Lane South). Stonework from the original buildings still survives in garden walls and rockeries.

Four Villages

Until the middle of the 19th century, 'Chiswick' was just the name of the riverside village on Chiswick Mall. It was one of four small villages in the area, the others being Little Sutton, Strand-on-the-Green and Turnham Green. Stamford Brook was a small hamlet at the eastern end of Turnham Green.

OLD CHISWICK

The village of Chiswick grew up along the riverside, around the parish church of St Nicholas, which is known to have been in existence since c.1181. Farming, fishing and other trades connected with the river were the main occupations of the inhabitants. No doubt the Chiswick ferry did brisk business from the merchants, pilgrims, preaching friars and others who travelled the medieval countryside, since there were no bridges across the Thames between London Bridge and Kingston Bridge until the eighteenth century.

The church was the centre of community life, serving as a clubhouse for secular as well as religious meetings, also as a theatre for the mystery plays.

From as early as the sixeenth century, Chiswick appears to have been a desirable country retreat for wealthy Londoners; its healthy reputation probably enhanced by the use of Chiswick manor house for Westminster School (see last chapter) 'in times of plague'. Noblemen built their mansions to the north and west of the church; other wealthy people built or rebuilt large and lovely houses along Chiswick Mall and up Church Street. The locals lived in a cluster of cottages around the church with the undignified name of Slut's Hole – rechristened Fisherman's Place by 1865.

In 1706, John Bowack, an early Chiswick historian, describes Chiswick thus: 'the town, tho' but small, is so very pleasantly situated, out of the road and free from traffic, noise and dust'.

Despite the substantial building and rebuilding of the eighteenth and early nineteenth centuries, the village spread very little until the later nineteenth century. It extended along the river from the church to the lime kiln at Hammersmith and north up Church Street, which turned left to meet Burlington Lane. Paul's (now Powell's) Walk provided a short cut to Burlington Lane and to Chiswick House. Lanes led

13. John Davidson cutting osiers on Chiswick Eyot in the 1920s. The osiers were used for making baskets.

14. St Nicholas church, Chiswick, and Slut's Hole, 1807, drawn by Schnebbelie.

through fields to link Chiswick with Turnham Green and Stamford Brook. The census of 1801 lists 1,023 inhabitants in Chiswick in 172 houses.

Chiswick also attracted industry: a medieval leather worker's dump was found in Pumping Station Road, there was a brewery from 1700 and by the nineteenth century, Thornycroft's had established its shipyard, the Chiswick Polish Company its factory and Chiswick Press its printing works (see pp84-92 for more details of industry).

Chiswick Eyot, the little island off Chiswick Mall, appears only to have been inhabited in prehistoric times. Osiers, a type of willow used for making baskets, were grown and harvested there from 1800. The Eyot, though, is being steadily washed away. It comprised four acres in the middle of the nineteenth century; 3¾ acres at the beginning of this century when it was a quarter of a mile long. Today it measures less than 300 yards. In the 1970s, Hounslow Council put forward a proposal to flatten it, since debris from its eroding banks was a nuisance to river traffic. Predictably there was an outcry; the island was saved and its banks shored up with concrete blocks in the 1980s. Home to many species of wild bird (a dolphin and a seal have also been seen there) it became a nature reserve in 1993.

LITTLE SUTTON

Although Sutton was the more important of the two medieval manors in Chiswick, the settlement that grew up around the manor house was probably never much more than a small, straggling hamlet in the loop of Sutton Lane – the bend in the road skirted a large fishpond now covered by Elmwood Road.

Agriculture would have been the main occupation of the inhabitants. Not only did they have to provide for themselves but they also had to do their stint for the manor. This meant ploughing in the winter and at Lent; harrowing; mowing; shearing and carting. Barley grew well in Chiswick so home-brewed ale was popular – documents tell us that nearly half the tenants in Sutton manor owed payment for making malt in 1222.

Known as Little Sutton by 1590, there were eleven ratepayers in 1630. In 1706 historian, John Bowack, dismisses it as 'a few poor houses which indeed do not deserve the name of a village'. There were cottages on the south of the bend – you can see one today: look for a small gabled white house as you travel along Cedars Road towards the M4. Although extensively modernised it dates to 1676. There was an inn, the Queen's Head (later nicknamed the Hole in the Wall – the name of the present pub); a dairy, run by Benjamin Tappenden 'bachelor and cowkeeper' from at least 1867 until it was sold to United Dairies in 1921. Sutton Court Farm, to the east of the manor house,

15. *Sutton Lodge, Heathfield Terrace, built in the mid nineteenth century, was a well-known Chiswick landmark. The local paper described it as 'a poor imitation of a Swiss chalet' when it was about to be demolished in 1956.*

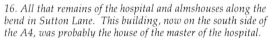

16. *All that remains of the hospital and almshouses along the bend in Sutton Lane. This building, now on the south side of the A4, was probably the house of the master of the hospital.*

was considered a model farm in 1794.

In 1845 historian, William Faulkner, described Little Sutton as still retaining a tranquil and retired character, well calculated to surprise visitors. Fifty years later much of the land was sold for redevelopment and the present roads and houses were built.

STRAND-ON-THE-GREEN

Described in 1932 as London's last remaining village, Strand-on-the-Green grew up as a small fishing settlement along the river bank. The name ('strand' probably means 'shore') was first recorded as 'Stronde' in 1353. It was called 'Strand Green' in 1593, and 'Strand under Green' in 1760.

The waterside path ran for 600m south-eastwards from the Kew ferry before turning inland to join Burlington Lane on the line of Grove Park Road. Most of the houses and workshops had entrances both on the river and from Back Lane (renamed Thames Road in 1907); alleyways connected Back Lane with the waterfront; orchards and fields lay behind until this century.

The opening of Kew Bridge in 1759 and the royal palace at Kew increased Strand's importance and popularity; large houses were built alongside the fishermen's cottages and small industries were set up on the waterfront. There were malt houses, boat

17. *Strand-on-the-Green under water in 1965. It is still prone to flooding.*

18. *Strand-on-the-Green, looking towards Kew Bridge, in 1832.*

19. *A malthouse at Strand-on-the-Green where barley was malted for the London market. There were at least five malthouses in Chiswick in the eighteenth century.*

repair yards, barge builders and wharves by 1865. The almshouses, first built in 1658, still remain. There were six pubs, a National School, and, by 1860, one of the largest laundries in London.

The City of London's Navigation Committee (later the Thames Conservancy Board) put up buildings on Oliver's island after 1777, and here barges were stationed for the collection of tolls. The last of the City ceremonial barges, the *Maria Wood*, was also berthed at Strand-on-the-Green. She was eighteen feet wide, 136ft long, flat bottomed and drawing only two feet of water; a resident writing in 1845 described her as 'the most conspicuous and pleasing object in this neighbourhood'.

Strand-on-the-Green began a slow decline in the nineteenth century when the Grand Junction Canal diverted freight traffic to Brentford and the Royal Family decamped from Kew to Windsor. Some industry remained until the 1950s but has now almost disappeared and Strand-on-the-Green has become a residential village again.

20. *The Maria Wood, last of the long line of barges built for the Lord Mayor of London, kept at Strand-on-the-Green. She was sold in 1859 and leased out for pleasure parties.*

21. *Turnham Green c.1790, by Samuel Hieronymous Grimm.*

22. The view across Turnham Green towards the Crown & Anchor in about 1831 (artist unknown), showing the pond at the eastern end of the Green.

23. Houses at the corner of Chiswick High Road and Acton Lane (demolished c.1894).

24. The remains of the village pound drawn in 1894, when it was no longer used. It stood on what is now Homefield Recreation Ground, opposite Balfern Grove.

TURNHAM GREEN

The village of Turnham Green grew up as a result of its position on the main road west. The name was first recorded in 1235 as 'Turneham' and 'Turnhamgrene' in 1396. No one knows what it means. It might be 'place in the bend of a river', or, perhaps, 'thorny place'.

The name was the subject of a rather bad pun at artist, Sir Joshua Reynold's dinner table. Spying some anaemic-looking peas, a wit called out to send "em to Hammersmith as that's the way to turn `em green'.

The Green, previously larger than today, was waste land of Sutton manor and a favourite haunt of footpads and highwaymen. William III was nearly assassinated nearby in 1696 (see p94) and the 7th Earl of Pembroke was involved in a bloody incident there in 1680. Pembroke and his party 'somewhat high flown with drink' were apprehended by a Constable of the Watch. Pembroke drew his sword, wounding the constable and killing a gentlemen who went to his assistance. At his trial Pembroke produced a King's Pardon and was discharged. Turnham Green was also the site of a famous skirmish during the Civil War.

There were ponds at both the western and eastern ends of the Green, around which animals grazed. Complaints were made about the state of the ponds in 1858 and they were filled in shortly afterwards. Small ponds on what is now the western side of Turnham Green Terrace, possibly the remains of gravel pits, are shown on a map of 1800. These were extended into a long expanse of water described as a 'canal' in the 1840s.

There was at least one smithy in Chiswick High Road and a pound for stray animals in Chiswick Lane (in Homefield Recreation Ground opposite Balfern Grove). A windmill stood somewhere near the junction of Windmill Road and Chiswick Common Road from about 1582. Nearby was the later workhouse, village lock-up and stocks. Several large pubs catered for travellers using the road. There were many small cottages – a survivor is the seventeenth-century (or even earlier) Arlington Cottages in Arlington Gardens, at the junction with Sutton Lane.

Substantial houses were built along the line of the High Road in the seventeenth century. John Bowack, writing in 1706, says of Turnham Green: 'there are several good brick houses and so considerable a number of inhabitants that it seems as big as Chiswick itself'. By the eighteenth century, the High Road from the Hammersmith boundary to the cross roads at Acton Lane was lined intermittently with large detached houses, many of which were later used as schools.

The only large eighteenth-century house still standing is Afton House in Bourne Place, now the Chiswick Memorial Club. Houses on the north side of the High Road included Bohemia House, at the top of Chiswick Lane, converted from the King of Bohemia public house and demolished in 1901; and Belmont House, just west of Boot's, demolished 1901. On the south side, set well back from the road: Sulhampstead House, between the present Devonshire and Annandale Roads, demolished 1880; Camden House, where the police station is now, demolished in the 1920s; Linden House, now the site of Linden Gardens, replaced in 1878 by another house and pulled down in the 1920s; and Bolton House, between Linden House and Afton House, which came down at the end of the nineteenth century.

Turnham Green remained mainly residential until the later nineteenth century. Pigot's *Middlesex Directory* of 1839-40 describes it as a neat village where 'very little business is carried out, the houses are truly respectable and chiefly inhabited by persons who have residence for trade in London, or by those retired from business'.

In the middle of the nineteenth century there was a large military barracks on the south side of the Green – the site now covered by the old Army and Navy furniture depository and the post office. The militia drilling on Turnham Green was 'the thing to watch' according to one resident.

The church on the Green, built in 1843, provided a focus for the community. This and other public buildings erected at the turn of the century – a fire station, police station, Town Hall, theatre and cinemas – together with shops and Sanderson's wallpaper fac-

25. *The oldest known photograph of Turnham Green, taken in 1863. The one-storey building on the left of the Crown & Anchor pub is a smithy; in front of it is a water pump.*

tory all combined to make Turnham Green the main administrative and commercial centre of the area we now call Chiswick. The High Road became busier after the introduction of electric trams in 1901.

STAMFORD BROOK

The small settlement of Stamford Brook (Stamford is a Saxon name meaning 'stone ford') grew up along the boundary of Chiswick and Hammersmith. This boundary also divided the old county of Middlesex from the county of London. Seven cottages are recorded at Stamford Brook in the 1630s, which, by 1733, had been incorporated into two larger houses. Of the four houses standing at Stamford Brook at the end of the eighteenth century, two still remain (see p37). Stamford Brook Common was a continuation of Turnham Green Back Common until separated by building in the later nineteenth century.

26. *This elegant early nineteenth-century terrace still remains, although it is hard to recognise now due to later buildings erected in its front gardens. It is Williams Terrace, Nos. 1-21 Chiswick High Road.*

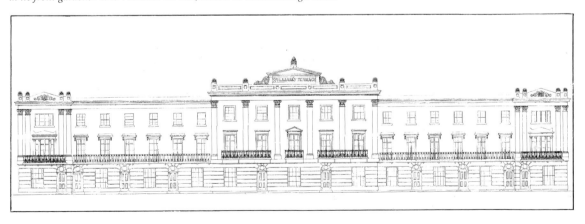

27. Old cottages on Back Common about 1825.

28. Linden House, one of the large houses which lined Chiswick High Road in the nineteenth century. Thomas Griffiths Wainewright, forger and poisoner (see p42) lived in Linden House.

Chiswick in the Civil War

THE STAND-OFF AT TURNHAM GREEN

Chiswick was thought to support the Royalist cause during the Civil War. In 1642 Parliamentarians burnt the altar rails of St Nicholas church, but they were prevented from going on to pillage the prebendal manor house on Chiswick Mall.

In November that year a decisive Civil War action took place on Turnham Green. It wasn't really a battle, more a skirmish, but an important one in that it foiled the King's attempt to retake London, which was in the hands of the Parliamentarians.

The Royalists, led by King Charles I's nephew, Prince Rupert of the Rhine, were marching on London from Oxford. They were halted at Brentford on 12 November by Parliamentary regiments, but after a fierce day's fighting, the Royalists won through.

Learning of the Battle of Brentford while sitting in the House of Lords (where he was giving Parliament an account of his campaigns), the leader of the Parliamentary army, the Earl of Essex, summoned his forces and marched to Turnham Green. Throughout the night regular soldiers and the Trained Bands of Lon-

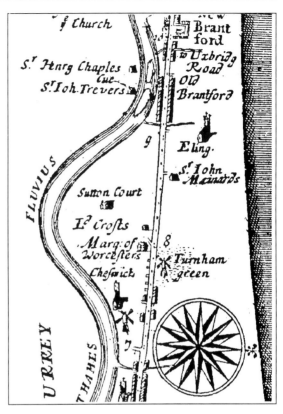

30. *Ogilby's road map, 1675, showing the windmill that stood on the north side of the High Road.*

29. *The Royalists and Parliamentarians in combat on Turnham Green, November 1642. This picture, painted by John Hassall, probably over-emphasises the violence of the action.*

31. The large pond on the western side of Turnham Green must have been an additional hazard for the Civil War soldiers. The pond had been filled in by 1864. The house behind it, called the Chestnuts, was demolished about 1904.

don apprentices poured out of London to Chiswick, along with 'cart loads of victuals'. By 8am, it is claimed, 24,000 Parliamentarian soldiers faced the Royalists who had arrived from Brentford.

The Parliamentarians sheltered behind hedges and in ditches, firing their muskets whenever the Royalist cavalry approached. But the ground wasn't suitable for horse soldiers and the Royalist foot soldiers were outnumbered two to one. So the Royalists gave up and retreated to Kingston in the evening. King Charles would never again come so close to taking his capital.

A contemporary account of the skirmish claims that 800 Royalist soldiers and 120 Parliamentarians were killed on Turnham Green but this is thought to be a gross exaggeration, mere Parliamentary propaganda.

IS CROMWELL BURIED AT CHISWICK?

In 1642 Oliver Cromwell was an MP and an as yet undistinguished army captain. He probably fought at the skirmish on Turnham Green, but there is no evidence for the claim that he held a military council in the Bulls Head, Strand-on-the-Green. He became Lord Protector of England in 1653, four years after the execution of King Charles, and when he died in 1658 his body was embalmed and buried in Westminster Abbey. Inevitably, his body was disinterred in 1661, after the Restoration, and hung on the gallows at Tyburn. The head was lopped off and set up on a pole

in Westminster Hall where it remained for over twenty years. The trunk was supposedly buried under the gallows, but persistent rumours suggest that Cromwell's children rescued the body and spirited it away.

Where did they take it? St Nicholas Church, Chiswick is one candidate. This claim rests on the fact that Cromwell's daughter, Mary, wife of Lord Fauconberg, lived at Sutton Court from 1676 until her death in 1713. She is buried in a vault inside the church, together with her sister Lady Frances Russell.

When the church was being rebuilt in 1882, the Fauconberg vault was opened and Captain Dale, the son of the vicar, claims it contained not two, but three, coffins. The third coffin, he said, appeared to have been subjected to 'rough usage'. Writing in the parish magazine fourteen years later, the vicar says no such sepulchre was found (there is some doubt, though, as to whether the vicar actually saw inside the vault).

Cromwell's biographers, however, think it more likely that the body was taken to Newburgh Priory, Fauconberg's home in the north of England, where a strange kiln-like tomb of brick still exists (it has never been opened). The Fauconbergs anyhow didn't move to Sutton Court until 15 years after Cromwell was disinterred. Whether or not Cromwell's headless body lies in the church is likely to remain a mystery since the Fauconberg vault is now covered with concrete many inches thick.

32. Grove House in 1792.

Grand Houses

London has always been a noisy, dirty, smelly place in which to live, where in earlier centuries plagues and other epidemics spread like wildfire. The 'sweet air and situation' of Chiswick, just six miles from Hyde Park Corner, was seen as a desirable country retreat from the sixteenth century onwards.

Apart from the manor houses of Sutton and Chiswick and the very large estate at Chiswick House (p45), there were several other sizeable mansions in Chiswick.

GROVE HOUSE
Grove House, known as the Grove Estate or Chiswick Grove in earlier times, stood on the western side of the present Kinnaird Avenue. A building is known to have been on the site since 1412; the house that was there in 1705 was described as a 'spacious regular modern building... pleasantly situated by the Thames side. Behind it are gardens by some said to be the finest in England'. Walnut trees and Spanish chestnuts were apparently their main features.

A family called Barker owned Grove House until 1745 when it was bought by the Earl of Grantham. He sold it to an eccentric politician called Humphrey Morice. Asses' milk was delivered to Morice during 1778-9. 'Delivered' meant that a poor little ass and her handler were obliged to trudge from Knightsbridge to Chiswick every day to produce half a pint of milk. Surprising really because Morice loved animals – when he died he bequeathed Grove House to a Mrs Luther 'on condition that all his animals were to be carefully fed until they died a natural death'.

In the 1840s the Duke of Devonshire acquired the estate. He remodelled the house, removing the upper storey, and let the house to tenants. The grounds were later developed as the Grove Park Estate.

The house itself remained until 1928. Its last owner was Lt Col Robert William Shipway, the saviour of Hogarth House, who bought it in the 1890s.

CORNEY HOUSE
Corney House, formerly Cornhythe, was on the river side, just west of St Nicholas Church, on the site of the Regency Quay development in Pumping Station Road. It was the home of the Russells (family name of the Earls of Bedford) from 1542 to 1663 and it was here that they entertained Queen Elizabeth I in 1602.

33. *Lt. Col. Shipway purchased Grove House in 1895. This was his entrance hall.*

When the family sold Corney House and moved to Bedford House on Chiswick Mall, the new owner rebuilt it. It was altered again in 1748 by James Gibbs and called Norfolk House. A later owner was George, Earl Macartney, diplomat and colonial governor, who died there in 1828. His widow sold out to the Duke of Devonshire who demolished it in 1832 and added the grounds to his own.

HEATHFIELD HOUSE

Heathfield House stood on the corner of Sutton Lane and Heathfield Terrace. There was a house there by at least 1659 but it only acquired the name 'Heathfield' in the eighteenth century when it was owned by General Eliott, created Lord Heathfield when, as Governor of Gibraltar, he defended the rock against a three-year siege by the Spanish.

Heathfield House was demolished in 1836 but its fine wrought iron entrance gates can still be seen: they are the gates that lead into Green Park from Piccadilly, opposite Half Moon Street.

34. *The gates leading into Green Park from Piccadilly, originally the gates to Heathfield House. When the house was demolished the gates were bought for Chiswick House by the Duke of Devonshire. In 1897 he moved them to his London home, Devonshire House in Piccadilly, and in 1921 they were bought for the Nation and set up at the entrance to Green Park.*

OTHER MANSIONS

There were many other large houses in Chiswick which have now disappeared. Sir Stephen Fox built three mansions in Chiswick in the late seventeenth century: in Burlington Lane, next to Chiswick House; in Chiswick Mall and on the west side of Chiswick Lane. The latter house was called the Manor Farm House and its garden walls can still be seen in Manor Alley and Ashbourne Grove and the house itself is illustrated on the sign of the Manor Tavern. It was popular with King William III, who on a visit de-

35. Corney House is shown on the left of this view of Chiswick from the river. It was painted by Jacob Knyff c.1658.

36. Stile Hall in 1890. This is the house that replaced that lived in by Johann Zoffany. It was demolished in 1892 to make way for Stile Hall Gardens.

clared: 'the place is perfectly fine, I could live here for five days'. Between 1786 and 1810, Manor Farm House was a school; later it was used for a mental asylum run by the Tuke family before being demolished in 1896.

At the very western end of Chiswick stood London Style House and Sydney House. The first, on the south corner of Wellesley Road, was rented to artist Johann Zoffany between 1764 and 1772, and the second, nearer the old Star and Garter pub, is said to be the house where Lady Mary Sydney, mother of Elizabethan poet, Sir Philip Sydney, retired in 1562 after being disfigured by smallpox. A later house, probably on this site, was called Stile Hall.

EXISTING HOUSES

One of the delights of Chiswick is that so much fine architecture survives, albeit somewhat altered. Chiswick Mall, particularly, has some splendid houses – the oldest house in Chiswick, the Old Burlington which dates to the sixteenth century, is discussed on p94.

Outstanding is Walpole House, at the eastern end of the Mall. This has features dating to the sixteenth and seventeenth centuries. The garden front dates to around 1700 and the river front and a north-west extension to c.1730. Famous residents include: Barbara Villiers, mistress of King Charles II; politician, Daniel O'Connell; Thomas Walpole (from whom the house took its name), the nephew of prime minister Sir Robert Walpole, and actor manager, Sir Herbert Beerbohm Tree.

In the early nineteenth century, Walpole House became an academy for young gentlemen, attended in 1817 by the young and homesick, William Makepeace Thackeray, lately returned from India. This was almost certainly the setting he had in mind for Miss Pinkerton's Seminary for Young Ladies in *Vanity Fair*, but considerable artistic licence was used in his illustration of Becky Sharp throwing her 'dixionary' out of the carriage window; a plaque on nearby Boston House also claims to be the venue. Thackeray probably used a composite of the two houses in his drawing.

Strawberry House, next door to Walpole, House was built c.1700 and refronted c.1730. Its finely proportioned cast iron porch was added towards the end of the eighteenth century. Morton House dates

37. Walpole House, Chiswick Mall, home to many famous people and at one time a school attended by William Makepeace Thackeray.

back to the seventeenth century at least. It was refronted in the 1730s but, when the bricks began to bulge in the 1950s, the facade was totally rebuilt – each brick, where possible, put back in its original position.

Bedford House and Eynham House at the western end of the Mall were originally one, and presumably the successor to the Bedford House occupied by the Russells in the 1660s. The present houses were built in the early eighteenth century. John Sich, founder of the Lamb Brewery, lived in Bedford House until his death in 1836. So did barrister and Chiswick historian, Warwick Draper. Tragically, Draper fell to his death from a balcony at Bedford House in 1926, while inspecting a chimney fire.

Further west, Woodroffe House dates from the late seventeenth century. A Woodroffe married his next door neighbour, a daughter of Thomas Plukenett who bought Bedford House from the Russells. This lucky lady subsequently inherited all the properties up to Chiswick Lane.

The Old Vicarage, on the corner of the Mall and Church Street, dates from 1657-8 when the old par-

38. Thackeray's illustration in Vanity Fair *of Becky Sharp throwing her 'dixionary' from the carriage window.*

39. Chiswick Mall in 1834, drawn by Havell, engraved by Cooke.

40. The Brook, Stamford Brook, leased by French artist, Lucien Pisarro in 1901 and bought in 1919. Members of the Pisarro family still live there. Drawing by Tom Parker.

sonage was pulled down and a new one built at a cost of £280 19s 5d (the house was refronted in the eighteenth century when the bow window was added).

Boston House in Chiswick Square (perhaps the smallest square in London) dates from the 1680s, but was extended and refaced in 1740 by Viscount Boston, later Earl of Grantham and resident of Grove House. It was sold in 1772 for £960, then described as 'the great house and offices...with a great parlour hung with green Embos'd Paper and Prints compleat'. Later still it became a school for young ladies, then a Roman Catholic sisterhood, when it was called Nazareth House.

Strand-on-the-Green also contains many old houses. No 65, Zoffany House, the later home of painter, Johann Zoffany, dates from the eighteenth century; No 1, Strand-on-the-Green House, built in the seventeenth century and refaced in 1788, was the setting for Margaret Kennedy's novel *The Constant Nymph*.

There are two eighteenth-century houses on Chiswick's eastern boundary: Stamford Brook House, which faces onto Stamford Brook Common, and The Brook, where artist Lucien Pisarro lived. The eastern wall of this house marked both the old Chiswick parish boundary with Hammersmith and the course of the Stamford Brook. The main house dates to the later seventeenth century but was bricked over a hundred years or so later.

Hogarth's house is discussed on p57 and some of the more interesting nineteenth and twentieth century houses on pp116-128.

41. Bedford House, Chiswick Mall. Michael Redgrave and his family lived here between 1945-54.

Illustrious People

According to John Bowack, Chiswick 'boasted more illustrious and noble persons than any of its neighbours'. That was in 1706 and illustrious people have been living in Chiswick ever since. Some of the more famous are mentioned here, others appear elsewhere in this book. Many well-known people still live in Chiswick but space doesn't allow for their inclusion.

ROYALTY
Chiswick lacks the royal connections of neighbouring Kew and Richmond, but royalty didn't bypass the place completely. Sutton Manor was a royal residence in the fourteenth and fifteenth centuries and Edward VII, when Prince of Wales, rented Chiswick House as a nursery residence for his young sons in the 1870s. He held a fête there for the Tsar of Russia, also attended by Queen Victoria.

NOBILITY
Titled names abound in the Chiswick records, and are reflected in many street names. The earls of Somerset

and Burlington; the dukes of Devonshire and the Duke of Monmouth (illegitimate son of Charles II), were all one-time residents of Chiswick House. Oliver Cromwell's son-in-law, Earl Fauconberg, lived at Sutton Court; the Russells (family name of the dukes of Bedford) at Corney House and Bedford House, Chiswick Mall; Lord Heathfield was at Heathfield House and the Duchess of Cleveland at Walpole House, Chiswick Mall.

Other titled inhabitants were the earls of Boston, Grantham, Portland, Warwick; marquesses of Worcester and Annandale and Viscount Shannon, and General Lord Fairfax.

Viscount Montgomery of Alamein spent part of his childhood at 19 Bolton Road, Grove Park and, at the age of 40, married Betty Carver at St Nicholas church on 27 July, 1927. His wife was an artist, who lived at 2 Riverside, Chiswick Mall. In 1945 Montgomery was made a Freeman of the Borough of Brentford and Chiswick.

STATESMEN
Two famous seventeenth-century Chiswick residents were Chaloner Chute (1595-1659) at Sutton Court, an MP and barrister who became Speaker of the House of Commons, and Sir Stephen Fox (1627-1716). Fox

42. *James, Duke of Monmouth, illegitimate son of Charles II and Lucy Walters. His father bought Chiswick House for him in 1664.*

43. *Field Marshal Montgomery lived in Grove Park as a child; married in St Nicholas church, and was made a Freeman of the borough of Brentford and Chiswick in 1945.*

44. *Sir Stephen Fox, seventeenth-century statesman, who bought Chiswick Prebendal Manor and put up houses and other buildings in Chiswick.*

45. *Johann Zoffany's portrait of the Misses Mary and Agnes Berry, friends and literary executors of Horace Walpole. When young they lived in the rebuilt Manor House on Chiswick Mall.*

was in the forefront of public affairs, holding several important posts including Paymaster General.

He became very wealthy. In 1680 his friend John Evelyn computed him to be worth £200,000 'honestly got and unenvied, which is next to a miracle'. Fox put his riches to good use, building churches, almshouses and charity schools in different parts of the country. In 1685 he purchased the copyhold estate of the Chiswick Prebendal Manor. He built three large mansions (see p.33), and put up a barn for the vicar, a lock-up and a pair of stocks. At the age of 77 he married for the second time and produced four more children.

More recently, Lord Grimond, leader of the Liberal Party from 1956-67, lived at 24 Priory Avenue, Bedford Park until his death in 1993.

ARTISTS

Many artists and craftspeople have been attracted to Chiswick, the most famous being William Hogarth (see p54).

The German-born portrait painter, Johann Zoffany (1733-1810), lived first at London Style House then at 65 Strand-on-the-Green. He presented an altar piece to St Nicholas church which, although considered 'inappropriate', hung there until the church was rebuilt when it was put away in the vestry before being sold at Christie's in 1904. He painted another trouble-

some altar piece in which the fishermen of Strand-on-the-Green served as models for a depiction of *The Last Supper*. This was designed for Kew church, but it was not accepted as Zoffany had modelled Judas on a prominent church member. Instead, Zoffany gave it to St George's church, Brentford and it now hangs in St Paul's Church, Brentford.

The French artist, printer and wood engraver, Lucien Pisarro (1863-1910), lived at 62 Bath Road, Bedford Park, then at The Brook, Stamford Brook. Lucien's father, impressionist painter Camille Pisarro, stayed with his son at 62 Bath Road in 1897 and painted six views from the house. Lucien also painted several pictures of Chiswick. He is perhaps better known for founding the Eragny Press which produced exquisite hand-printed books.

The many artistic residents of Bedford Park, nicknamed the 'Bohemian Brotherhood of the Brush', included Cecil Aldin (1870-1935), prolific illustrator and artist who lived in Flanders Road and Priory Road. Most famous for his pictures of dogs, Aldin owned plenty of animal models himself: at one time thirteen dogs, two monkeys and a fox cub. He drove himself around in a donkey and cart and regularly set off on his horse to hunt at Esher.

J.C. Dollmann, painter of *A Very Gallant Gentleman*, the picture depicting Captain Oates stumbling out into the snow to die during Scott's Antarctic expedition, lived at 12/14 Newton Grove. Watercolourist, T.M. Rooke (he painted the original sign for The Tabard, Bedford Park) at 7 Queen Anne's Gardens; Sir William Russell Flint, 12 Bedford Road, and architects, E.J. May at 6 Queen Anne's Grove, Maurice Adams at 14 Woodstock Road and 1 Marlborough Crescent, and C.F.A. Voysey at 7 Blandford Road.

Engraver, William Sharp (1749-1824), lived on Chiswick Mall and, before moving to nearby Kelmscott House in 1879, William Morris rented Horrington House on Chiswick High Road, near Thornton Avenue, in 1872.

WRITERS

Poet and essayist, Alexander Pope (1688-1744), is more usually associated with Twickenham, but for two years from 1716 he lived with his parents in Mawson Row, Old Chiswick 'under the wing of my Lord Burlington' – the house is now the Mawson Arms pub. Some of Pope's original translation of *The*

46. *Woodcut of the Eragny Press, founded by Lucien Pisarro.*

47. *Cecil Aldin driving his donkey cart in Queen Anne's Gardens, Bedford Park in 1898.*

48. Alexander Pope, who lived with his parents in Mawson Row, Old Chiswick (the house is now the Mawson Arms pub). Pope's father is buried in St Nicholas churchyard.

49. The Said House, Chiswick Mall, with its large curved glass window, put in by Sir Nigel Playfair who owned the house in the 1930s.

Iliad was drafted on the back of letters addressed to 'Mr Pope at his house in ye New Buildings, Chiswick'.

Novelist, Samuel Richardson lived as a copyhold tenant of Sutton Court manor from 1736-1738. Italian poet, Ugo Foscolo (1776-1827) spent the last months of his life at Bohemia House (see p.26) and was buried in St Nicholas churchyard, but in 1871 his remains were taken to Florence. Playwright Arthur Wing Pinero (1855-1934) lived at 10 Marlborough Crescent, Bedford Park.

The Yeats family: father J.B. Yeats, painter, and his two sons: poet, W.B. Yeats, and artist, Jack Yeats lived at 8 Woodstock Road, Bedford Park, and after some years in Ireland at 3 Blenheim Road, Bedford Park from 1888-1900.

Novelist, E.M. Forster had a *pied à terre* in 9 Arlington Park Mansions, Sutton Lane; Stephen Potter, author of *Gamesmanship, One-upmanship* etc, lived on Chiswick Mall; Alun Owen, playwright responsible for the script of the Beatles' film *A Hard Day's Night*, in Upham Park Road; Nancy Mitford, who wrote *The Pursuit of Love* and *Noblesse Oblige* lived at Rose Cottage, Strand-on-the-Green between 1933 and 1936. Jerrard Tickell (author of *Odette, Appointment with Venus*) lived at 2 The Moorings, Strand-on-the-Green for a while.

ACTORS

Joe Miller (1684-1738), a well-known comedian of his time lived at Strand-on-the-Green. He became better known the year after his death when a *Joe Miller's Jest Book* was published. Charles Holland (1733-69), actor and son of a local baker, was cut off in his prime by smallpox. The epitaph on his tomb in St Nicholas churchyard was penned by David Garrick.

Poor William Terris (1847-97), actor and resident of 2 Bedford Road, Bedford Park, was stabbed at the stage door of the Adelphi Theatre before giving a performance. His murderer was found guilty but insane.

Two famous actor-managers, Sir Herbert Beerbohm Tree (1853-1917) and Sir Nigel Playfair (1874-1935), both lived on Chiswick Mall, the former in Walpole House and the latter, who revived the Lyric Theatre, Hammersmith, in The Said House.

Impresario C.B. Cochran lived in Esmond Road, Bedford Park; Michael Redgrave and his family owned Bedford House, Chiswick Mall between 1945-1954. Michael Flanders (of Flanders and Swann fame) lived at 63 Esmond Road, comedian Tommy Cooper in Barrowgate Road, and actor Donald Pleasance at Strand-on-the-Green; television personality Eamonn Andrews lived in Hartington Road.

50. *The seventeenth-century alabaster monument to Sir Thomas Chaloner in St Nicholas church.*

51. *Thomas Griffiths Wainewright drew this self portrait when a convict in Tasmania.*

OTHERS

The most remarkable monument in St Nicholas church is that of Sir Thomas Chaloner the younger (1561-1615). Chaloner was the Chamberlain of the household of James I, a naturalist and the first person to mine alum (a salt used for various things) in Britain.

Architect and landscape designer, Willam Kent, lived with the Burlingtons in Chiswick House and traveller Sir John Chardin (1643-1712), at Turnham Green. Dr William Rose, who kept a school called Bradmore House in Chiswick Lane, must have been a charismatic character: Dr Johnson used to visit him regularly, and philosopher, Jean-Jacques Rousseau actually took lodgings with a grocer in Chiswick to be near Dr Rose.

A TRIPLE MURDERER?

Chiswick's most notorious resident was probably Thomas Griffiths Wainewright who lived at Linden House, Turnham Green. He was an artist and art critic whose friends included Hazlitt, De Quincey and Charles Lamb. He was also a dandy, described as an 'over dressed young man', a spendthrift, a forger and a probable poisoner.

Wainewright was born at Linden House in 1794 and brought up by his grandfather, Dr Ralph Griffiths, editor of *The Monthly Review.* In 1826 Wainewright's bachelor uncle, George Edward Griffiths, invited Wainewright and his wife to return to live in Linden House. Six months later, Uncle George became suddenly and unaccountably ill, seized with convulsive stomach pains and died in terrible agony. Wainewright inherited the house and later his mother-in-law died in just the same way (according to the nurse who attended both death beds) six days after making a will leaving her estate to her eldest daughter, Wainewright's wife.

That same year, Helen Abercromby, Wainewright's 21-year-old sister-in-law, was urged by Wainewright to take out a two-year insurance policy on her life – not with one insurance company, but with several – the proceeds in the event of death to go to her sister and the Wainewrights. To escape his debtors, Wainewright and his entourage moved to Conduit Street. There, the young and previously healthy Helen was taken ill and died a week later. The doctors were persuaded that the cause of death was wet feet and too many oysters.

The insurance companies thought the death suspicious and refused to pay out on the policies. Undeterred, Wainewright sued one of the companies. The case came to court five years later and the insurance company won. Wainewright, meanwhile, had taken refuge in France. Nobody knows what he did there but it is rumoured that he spent some months in a Paris gaol on a charge of having poison in his possession for which he couldn't account.

When he returned to England seven years after Helen Abercromby's death he was promptly arrested – not for murder, but for bank forgery, a crime he had committed eleven years earlier when he forged his cousins' signatures to get his hands on a capital sum to which he wasn't entitled. He was convicted and transported to Tasmania where he died in 1847.

While in prison awaiting trial, Wainewright is said to have admitted to the murders, which it is thought were caused by the poisons strychnine and antimony.

CHISWICK GHOSTS

Barbara Villiers, Duchess of Cleveland and long time mistress of Charles II is reputed to haunt Walpole House on Chiswick Mall where she lived for the last two, sad years of her life. She was a remarkable and beautiful woman but became afflicted with dropsy and swelled to 'a monstrous bulk'. The tap, tap of her high heels is said to have been heard on the stairs, and her mournful bloated face seen, pressed against a window, with hands clasped in despair, pleading for the return of her lost beauty. However, the present owner of Walpole House, who has lived there for nearly fifty years, is not convinced.

The ghost of Boston House, Chiswick Square is, appropriately, Lady Boston. When her husband discovered her dalliance with near-neighbour General Lord Fairfax, he murdered her and took her body down a dark passage which led from the house to the river. But the body was washed up by the tide a few days later and buried with great secrecy in a corner of the garden. There have been sightings of a woman in a long dress, with hands outstretched and great terror written on her face. When the Chiswick Polish Company owned the house a large annexe containing a

52. *Barbara Villiers, Duchess of Cleveland and mistress of Charles II. Her ghost is said to haunt Walpole House, Chiswick Mall.*

staff restaurant was built over Lady Boston's grave – the Company's workers in the 1920s are said to have seen the ghost.

The Old Burlington in Church Street, once an Elizabethan ale house (see p.94) is said to have a ghost named Percy, described as 'good humoured and harmless'. Dressed in a wide brimmed hat and a long cloak, he is thought to have been a highwayman.

A poltergeist was reported in Esmond Road in July 1956 when a couple and their thirteen-year-old son were driven from their house by penny pieces flying through the air. This onslaught started the week after the family moved to the house. Wherever the boy went, pennies, and, later, razor blades, clothes pegs and even a spanner flew about. 'It was as if he was magnetised' said his mother. The house was exorcised and the poltergeist activity ceased.

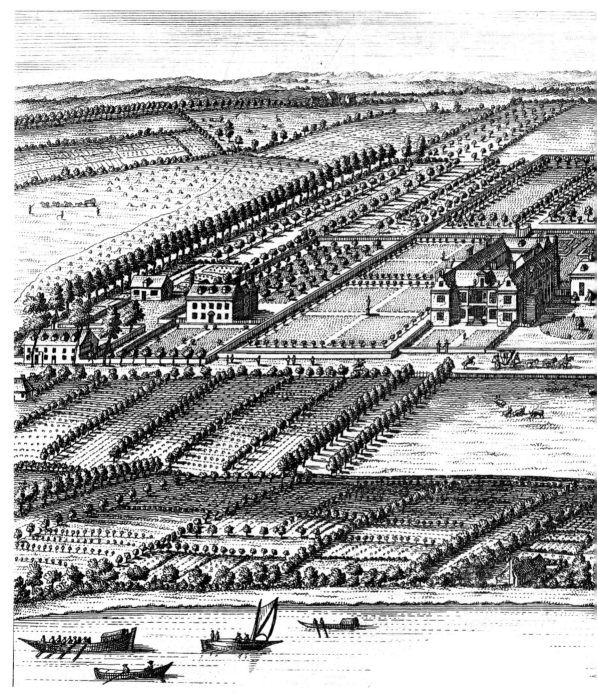

53. The Jacobean house, in the centre of the picture, in c.1700, by Leonard Knyff. The stable block is on the right.

Chiswick House

Chiswick House, the villa built by the Earl of Burlington between 1727-9, is one of the finest Palladian-style buildings in Britain. It also pioneered a shift in architectural fashion, away from the baroque style of Wren and Vanbrugh towards classical/renaissance architecture.

Visitors to Chiswick House are frequently surprised at its small size, strange layout and lack of kitchens or other service areas. But Chiswick House was not initially designed as a home to live in; it was the adjunct of another much larger house. Understanding the history of the two houses helps interpret the Chiswick House we see today.

THE JACOBEAN HOUSE

A house was built on land belonging to the prebendal manor probably about 1610 for Sir Edward Wardour. He sold the house to Robert Carr, the disgraced Earl of Somerset, who either retired there – or was banished – after being implicated in a murder. Later owners included the Earl of Pembroke and the Duke of Monmouth. In 1682 it was sold to the 1st Earl of Burlington and later inherited by his 10-year-old great-grandson Richard Boyle, the 3rd Earl, in 1704. He was the 'Architect Earl' and designer of the present Chiswick House.

The old house was built to a traditional plan, arranged around four sides of a courtyard. The 2nd Earl added a fine stable block (later known as the Grosvenor wing, this was not demolished until 1933). As the picture opposite shows, the house that stood on the site in 1700 was handsome. John Bowack, in 1706, described it as 'a noble and ancient seat... with many very spacious rooms in it and large gardens behind it'. After the house was damaged by fire in 1725 the 3rd Earl altered the facade.

This house was the Chiswick home of the Burlingtons and their successors, the dukes of Devonshire, until, in 1788, the 5th Duke of Devonshire demolished it and added two wings (now gone) to the present villa to provide living and kitchen accommodation.

54. Portrait of the young Richard Boyle, 3rd Earl of Burlington, by Jonathan Richardson. The garden building called the Bagnio, Burlington's first design, is shown in the background.

55. William Kent, Burlington's landscape designer and friend.

THE EARL OF BURLINGTON

Richard Boyle, 3rd Earl of Burlington was a man of wealth and taste, a great patron to artists, architects and musicians, and a holder of important posts at the court of George I. He was also an architect himself, designing several buildings as well as Chiswick House. His architectural style was inspired by his great love of the buildings of Classical Rome and his admiration of architects like Andrea Palladio and Inigo Jones.

Like any young nobleman, Burlington went on the Grand Tour, and in Italy first met William Kent (1685-1748) artist, architect and landscape designer. In 1719 Burlington brought Kent back from Italy and installed him in an apartment in Burlington House, Piccadilly. This was the start of a life-long friendship and artistic collaboration. Kent was to live with the Burlingtons for the rest of his life and is buried in St Nicholas church.

Kent and Burlington were an odd combination – a real attraction of opposites. Burlington, wealthy nobleman, learned scholar and rigid theorist, Kent, humbly-born, impulsive, and mercurial. However, the letters between them show a friendship full of humour and affection. Kent was a great favourite with Lady Burlington too. She nicknamed him 'the little Signor' and took painting lessons from him.

Kent probably played little part in the design of Chiswick House itself, although he is thought to have been responsible for some of the interior decoration, the painted ceilings particularly. But he had a large hand in the landscaping of the gardens. Horace Walpole maintained that it was Kent who first saw that 'all nature was a garden'.

As soon as he came of age Burlington began modifying his properties in Piccadilly, Londesborough and Chiswick and acquiring more land for the grounds of the latter. He first worked on the gardens of the Jacobean mansion, before building the villa in the garden (now called Chiswick House), 18 metres south west of the main house.

In 1733 Lord and Lady Burlington resigned all their court appointments, moved their pictures from Burlington House (now the core building of the Royal Academy) and made Chiswick their main London seat. Lord Burlington was disaffected: he had failed to secure a promised court appointment and was opposed to the Excise Bill. Work continued on the houses and gardens. What is now known as the Link Building was put up to connect the two Chiswick houses. The old Summer Parlour was turned into Lady Burlington's Garden Room 'at her own expence' and a gateway, designed by Inigo Jones, one of

Burlington's mentors brought from the demolished Beaufort House, Chelsea. Pope wrote a poem to the gate:

> I was brought from Chelsea last year
> Batter'd with wind and weather
> Inigo Jones put me together
> Sir Hans Sloane left me alone
> Burlington brought me hither.

Pope was a great friend and admirer of Lord Burlington to whom he dedicated the fourth of his *Moral Essays*. Horace Walpole, also a fan, said of Burlington 'He possessed every quality of genius except envy'. But next door neighbour, William Hogarth, couldn't stand Burlington, Kent and their ilk and satirised them wickedly (see p.56).

Burlington died at Chiswick in 1753 and was buried in the family vault of his northern seat, Londesborough in Yorkshire.

THE GROUNDS

Burlington's love of the classical extended to his garden design. He abandoned the formal layout of the Jacobean house gardens and attempted to create the type of garden that would have been found in a suburb of Ancient Rome: greenery and water interspersed with statues and architecture. Diagonal avenues were laid out through a wilderness, each terminating in a small building. One of these garden buildings was the young Earl's first architectural venture.

Closely supervised by architect, Colen Campbell, Burlington designed a 'bagnio' (bath house). Now gone, it was a fairly substantial building with a frontage of 37ft, four rooms on the ground floor, a large salon above and probably a cold bath in the basement. Burlington used it as his drawing office.

The Bollo Brook, which initially formed the southwest boundary of the estate, was canalised, then turned into a lake. A temple was built by the water with a sunken amphitheatre, pool and obelisk in front. Orange trees in tubs were placed on the steps of the amphitheatre.

When Burlington acquired land on the other side of the water in 1726 and 1727 a new entrance was laid out from Burlington Lane along an elevated terrace and across a watersplash by a cascade. Water was supposed to gush out of the cascade, powered by engines from a tall octagonal tower, probably on the site of the present junction of Burlington Lane/Chertsey Road/Edensor Road. Sadly, the cascade never seems to have worked properly. Daniel Defoe reveals that it failed hydraulically in 1742 and the problems were still being addressed in 1746.

Kent appears to have become involved with the gardens after 1733. He was largely responsible for laying out the new land and, using his painter's eye, knitting the whole landscape design together. It was a revolutionary garden in its day, the huge sweeps of lawn particulary being described as 'a new taste in gardening'

56. The Ionic Temple and the Orange Tree Garden.

THE PALLADIAN VILLA

Burlington's villa combines classical elements, modelled on the buildings of Ancient Rome and the architectural drawings of Andrea Palladio and Inigo Jones (of which he was an avid collector), with renaissance and baroque elements. Horace Walpole described it as 'a model of taste but not without faults some of which are occasioned by too strict adherence to rules and symmetry.' Indeed, Burlington did everything by the book – every single detail outside and in is based on precedent. Nothing is left to chance. However, the end result is a neo-classical *tour de force*.

The two-storeyed house is almost square with eight unusual obelisk-style chimneys and outside staircases back and front leading to the upper storey. There is a Corinthian portico on the front which is flanked by statues of Burlington's heroes, Palladio and Jones.

Today visitors enter on the rather catacomb-like lower level with its plain Tuscan-style rooms. Burlington had his library here, and the entrance hall was probably used as a waiting room for business visitors, but otherwise no one knows how these rooms were used originally. Although there is a wine cellar there were no kitchens and the fact that there is only a narrow spiral staircase to the upper storey suggests it was never the intention to serve meals from below, or for guests to be entertained here – the spiral staircase certainly would have posed difficulties for ladies in hooped skirts.

Guests in Burlington's day would have entered the house by the outside staircase leading to the upper floor. This is where the house comes to life with its octagonal domed hall, long gallery and six rooms of novel shapes, all lavishly decorated.

Burlington has left no record of his intentions in building Chiswick House. More beautiful than convenient, it was perhaps just an architectural study. Some people think it could have been a masonic temple. More likely it was to provide a sumptuous setting in which to display his books, paintings and sculptures and to entertain sophisticated company – a temple of the arts.

SEAT OF THE DEVONSHIRES

On Lord Burlington's death Chiswick House passed into the hands of the dukes of Devonshire through the marriage of Burlington's only surviving daughter. It remained their property until 1929. The 5th Duke and his popular, charismatic wife, society queen, Georgiana, spent a great deal of time at Chiswick, entertaining their Whig friends who included playwright Richard Brinsley Sheridan and politician Charles James Fox. Fox died at Chiswick House in 1806, while Foreign Secretary.

57. *Three walks in the gardens of Chiswick House, each terminated by a small building.*

58. *The two Chiswick houses viewed from Burlington Lane in c.1733.*

59. The gateway designed by Inigo Jones for Beaufort House, Chelsea, brought to Chiswick House in 1737.

The 5th Duke also made some major changes: in 1788 the Jacobean mansion was demolished and two wings, designed in the Palladian style, added to what is now Chiswick House. They contained the service and living accommodation which transformed the house into a real country mansion.

Alterations were also made to the gardens and the wooden bridge over the canal replaced by the present stone classical bridge, designed by James Wyatt in 1774.

The 6th Duke, who inherited the house in 1811, was no slouch when it came to developing his estate and acquired a great deal of neighbouring property. On the east, the Italian gardens were laid out by Lewis Kennedy, of the Lee & Kennedy horticultural firm based in Hammersmith, and the great greenhouse designed by Samuel Ware put up. The Duke also constructed Duke's Avenue as a northern entrance to his house, another entrance to the south, and obtained an Act of Parliament in 1818 to re-route Burlington Lane further away from the property.

He also laid on some very lavish entertainments. Distinguished visitors included Tsar Alexander and the King of Prussia in 1814, Queen Victoria in 1842, Tsar Nicholas I and the king of Saxony in 1844. George Canning, while Prime Minister, died at Chiswick House in 1827.

The Duke kept a menagerie of exotic animals. The sight of his tame elephant and giraffes cavorting about the grounds no doubt enlivened these 'fêtes'. The giraffes (some of the first to be brought to England) were kept in a special house and paddock on what is now Upham Park Road and their ponderous progress through Turnham Green must have amused the residents.

60. *Chiswick House from the front, after the wings were added in 1788.*

61. *Visitors inspecting the giraffes kept by the 6th Duke of Devonshire in the grounds of Chiswick House.*

62. When T.A. Greeves drew this sketch of Chiswick House in 1958, the wings had recently been demolished and the Link Building was in the process of being resurrected on the right-hand side of the house.

LATER HISTORY

The 6th Duke died in 1858, and left the house to his sister, the dowager Countess Granville, for the remainder of her life. After her death it was let to various tenants including the future Edward VII. In 1892 Chiswick House became a mental home until in 1929 the estate was bought by Middlesex County Council to prevent the 9th Duke of Devonshire redeveloping it, and leased to Brentford and Chiswick Urban District Council, which opened the grounds to the public.

However, the house fell into disrepair and in 1948 was acquired by the Ministry of Works, which began a ten-year restoration programme. The two eighteenth-century wings were taken down (many consider this to be an act of architectural vandalism) to expose Lord Burlington's villa. The Link Building and the Summer Parlour, however, were resurrected from behind the wings. Although built by Lord Burlington, the Summer Parlour was really part of the old house and the Link Building was designed merely to connect the two houses. Today they stand in line, with no function and leading absolutely nowhere, thus distorting the shape of the Palladian villa originally conceived by the Architect Earl.

Chiswick House was opened to the public in 1958. It is now in the care of English Heritage, while Hounslow Council is responsible for the grounds.

63. Scene from A Rake's Progress *by Hogarth, which tells the story of a young rake who squanders his inheritance on high living only to meet a tragic end in the madhouse at Bedlam. Here, the rake's sedan chair is being waylaid by bailiffs pressing him for outstanding debts.*

Hogarth and his Little Country Box

William Hogarth (1697-1764), the quintessential English painter and engraver, best known for his prints satirising everyday life, bought himself what he described as 'a little country box ' in Chiswick in 1749. For the remainder of his life he spent the greater part of each summer here and is buried in the graveyard of St Nicholas church.

Hogarth House, Hogarth Lane is now a Hogarth museum. In the nineteenth century the house was described as standing in 'a narrow, dirty lane'. Today that 'lane' is part of the wide, noisy A4.

WILLIAM HOGARTH

The son of a not very successful classical scholar turned schoolmaster and bookseller's hack, William Hogarth was born in Bartholomew Close, City of London. At the age of fifteen he was apprenticed to a silver-plate engraver and shortly after completing his apprenticeship, he set up in business on his own. Run-of-the-mill work was the engraving of trade cards, coats of arms and designs onto plate, but before long he began to produce the distinctive prints which were to make his name and his fortune.

Hogarth produced nearly 300 engravings, prints from which were sold for modest prices. The most famous are his 'Modern Moral' narrative essays such as *A Harlot's Progress*, *Marriage à la Mode* and *A Rake's Progress*, which expose the follies and foibles of eighteenth-century London. They are a pictorial satire of

avarice, coarseness, crudity, corruption, debauchery, quackery, pretentiousness and other unattractive features of life of that (or any other) time.

His prints were immediately popular, so much so that they were widely pirated. Hogarth campaigned vigorously to 'secure my property to myself'. He succeeded in 1735 when the Engravers Copyright Act was introduced. Called 'Hogarth's Act', this forbade people to copy an engraving without the designer's permission. It was the first Copyright Act in British law.

Hogarth was a serious painter as well as a caricaturist, but the commercial success of his engravings interfered with his reputation. There was little interest in his historical/religious compositions or his portraits. Even more unpopular was *The Analysis of Beauty*, the book outlining his views on art, at which he laboured long and hard. His friends disliked it and his enemies ridiculed it.

Hogarth was ambitious not just for himself but for the position of artists in English society. Fiercely independent, cocky and belligerent, he made many enemies. Unfriendly caricaturists, detecting the snub-nosed, heavy-jowled likeness between Hogarth and his pug dog Trump nicknamed him 'Painter-Pugg'.

Hogarth was one of the most significant artists of the eighteenth century but he never received proper

64. *William Hogarth, by G.M. Brighty, published in 1817.*

65. *Hogarth's tomb in St Nicholas Churchyard with the river beyond.*

acknowledgement in his own time and died embittered. Even when he auctioned off the original canvasses from which he made his comic engravings only one person made a bid. That person acquired some of the best pictorial satire ever for a mere 120 guineas.

Hogarth was at Chiswick the night before he died in his London home in Leicester Square. His famous tomb in St Nicholas churchyard, topped by a classical urn (described as 'a tea caddy'), was erected by a group of friends in 1771. The inscription was written by David Garrick. It reads:

Farewell, great painter of mankind
Who reached the noblest point of art
Whose pictured morals charm the mind
And through the eye correct the heart.

If genius fire thee, Reader, stay;
If Nature touch thee, drop a tear;
If neither move thee, turn away,
For Hogarth's honoured dust lies here.

HOGARTH AND LORD BURLINGTON

In his desire to establish a native style of English art and to improve the status of English artists, Hogarth was out of step with the aesthetic preferences of the time, which favoured all things Continental. Artistic

66. Hogarth's only picture of Chiswick. The drawing was probably made from the river looking towards Burlington Lane and the print is possibly a reverse of the original etching. Mr Ranby's house is the centre foreground; the large mansion on the right may be the house belonging to the then Earl of Northampton, the dome on the far right could be Chiswick House.

67. This print attributed to Hogarth shows the 'gate of good taste' with Alexander Pope (A) and Lord Burlington (F) attempting to whitewash it, and in the process splattering whitewash on Lord Chandos (B), who was patron of Hogarth's father-in-law.

68. Hogarth Lane, with Hogarth House on the right in 1897. Watercolour by T.M. Rooke.

tastes were dictated by the art patrons of the day, one of the greatest of whom was Lord Burlington, Hogarth's near neighbour in Chiswick.

Lord Burlington and his set were the epitome of all Hogarth despised: 'imitators and mannerists' he called them and didn't hesitate to lampoon them in his prints. In the background of *Masquerades and Operas* is Lord Burlington's Piccadilly Mansion, giving aristocratic sanction to the taste of the London crowd. It is labelled 'ACADEMY OF ARTS' – a citadel of false taste.

Another print entitled *The Burlington Gate*, attributed to Hogarth, shows Lord Burlington himself with his friends William Kent and Alexander Pope. The extravagantly Italianate Kent was Hogarth's real *bête noir:* 'never was there a more wretched dauber' he said. In the two prints mentioned above, Kent is shown above the portal of Burlington Gate, in the pose of a Roman Emperor with palette and paintbrush, receiving admiring glances from Michelangelo and Raphael. Hogarth's dislike of Kent probably had a lot to do with the fact that Kent had replaced Hogarth's father-in-law, the talented history painter

James Thornhill, as painter to Kensington Palace.

Chiswick itself features in only one of Hogarth's pictures – the etching, shown here, known as *View of Mr Ranby's House*. Mr Ranby was surgeon to the royal household for whom Hogarth painted portraits of his children.

HOGARTH'S HOUSE

The narrow, brick and tiled house dates to about 1700. The distinctive triple bay window in the Best Parlour was added by Hogarth. Every room beneath the attic has wood-panelling from floor to ceiling.

In the walled garden the stable with loft above (which Hogarth used as a studio) is no longer there, nor is the avenue of filbert trees in which Hogarth played ninepins, or the graves of a pet bird and a dog ('Alas, Poor Dick! 1760. Aged 11' read the headstone of the former). However, the mulberry tree at the front of the house remains. Mulberry tarts made from the fruit of this very tree were given to the local children when they came to visit. Hogarth loved dogs and children and was one of the founder-governors

69. *Hogarth House from the garden with the mulberry tree in the foreground. Mrs Hogarth made mulberry tarts from the fruit of this tree for local children. It still bears fruit today.*

of the Foundling Hospital in Bloomsbury established by philanthropist Thomas Coram.

After Hogarth's death, the house was occupied by Hogarth's wife, Jane followed by members of her family until 1808 when it was sold. It was allowed to fall into decay and when it came on the market in 1900 attempts were made to raise money to buy it through public subscription. They failed, the whole of Chiswick parish contributing only £12. Lt Col Robert Shipway of Grove House stepped in to buy it, restored it, and opened it to the public in 1902.

Colonel Shipway bought a shell – none of Hogarth's pictures or possessions remained. Furniture in the style of the period was commissioned from the Chiswick Artworkers Guild and 130 Hogarth prints acquired.

Colonel Shipway conveyed Hogarth House to the Middlesex County Council in 1909 to be used as a Hogarth Museum. It was badly bombed in 1940 but was repaired and re-opened in 1951. The house was transferred to the Borough of Hounslow in 1965.

Chiswick on the Move

BY WATER

Road travel was a hazardous business until the nineteenth century, so, where possible, it was cleaner, cheaper and more convenient to use the river. The only obstacles for traffic were the fishing weirs arranged in a zig zag pattern across the Thames – these became such a nuisance that they were eventually abolished.

There would have been a continual stream of traffic along the Thames by Chiswick: people going about their business in wherries, fishing boats and other small craft; barges loading and unloading provisions; grander craft belonging to the owners of riverside mansions, docking at their own watergates. Later there were steamboats. The first regular steam packet

service to operate on this stretch of river – from Queenhithe to Twickenham – began in 1824.

Today the river presents a rather forlorn spectacle on a riverside walk, except on Boat Race Day, but in earlier centuries there would have been plenty of entertainment. It might only have been an overloaded boat capsizing in mid-stream, but it could have been a glimpse of sumptuous velvets and rich brocades as royal personages glided down the Thames in magnificent barges to palaces at Kew, Richmond, Hampton Court and Windsor, or the sight of the Lord Mayor's old barge, the *Maria Wood* which had its winter moorings opposite Strand-on-the-Green.

The Chiswick foreshore would have provided a grandstand view of the many ceremonies and processions that took place on the river. Like the huge coronation procession of King Henry VII's queen, Elizabeth of York, from Richmond on 30 November 1487; or the state entry into London of Charles II and Queen Catherine in 1662. The barge they took from Kew was covered in cloth of gold and festooned with flowers.

70. The ferry boat from Chiswick to Barnes with St Nicholas church and Chiswick Mall in the background. The ferry continued to run until the 1930s.

71. *The first Kew Bridge, opened 1759. It was the only bridge across the Thames between Fulham and Kingston until Richmond Bridge opened in 1777.*

CROSSING THE RIVER

It can still be a nightmare getting across the Thames: imagine what it must have been like before the bridges were built. In early times travellers had no choice but to cross by ford or ferry. The nearest known fording point was at Brentford.

A ferry at Chiswick is first mentioned in a document dated 1659, although it's hard to believe it wasn't in use much earlier. Maps of the early nineteenth century show that the ferry left from the end of Chiswick Lane (now Chiswick Lane South) but later in the century it moved further down Chiswick Mall to Church Walk by St Nicholas church. The ferry continued in use until the 1930s.

Another ferry ran from Kew to the western edge of Strand-on the-Green until it was replaced by the first Kew Bridge. The latter was a wooden structure, built by Robert Tunstall, a Brentford businessman. There was no opposition to it from the ferry owners at Strand-on-the-Green and Brentford, which is hardly surprising since Tunstall owned them both.

Opened in June 1759 (3,000 people crossed it on the first day), Kew Bridge was the only bridge between Fulham and Kingston. It wasn't cheap: the toll for a coach and four was 1s 6d (7½p), and a foot passenger paid a halfpenny.

After a boat collided with, and damaged, the wooden bridge, Robert Tunstall's son replaced it with a stone bridge in 1789. This was inaugurated by George III and 'a great concourse of carriages'. Tolls were discontinued when it was sold to the Metropolitan Board of Works for £57,300 in 1873.

The structure of the second bridge wasn't considered strong enough when increased traffic necessitated its widening at the end of the nineteenth century and it was replaced by the present bridge in 1903. Designed by Sir John Wolfe Barry (who was the engineer for Tower Bridge) the bridge is 55ft wide and 1,182ft long. It was opened by Edward VII in whose honour it was named, but the name doesn't appear to have caught on and it quickly reverted to plain Kew Bridge. A map of the Kew area found by Allied forces in Germany at the end of the war suggests that Kew Bridge was high on the German hit list – shrapnel marks can be seen on the stonework.

Chiswick's second road bridge, Chiswick Bridge, built to take the new Great Chertsey Road across the river, was opened in 1933 by the Prince of Wales. Designed by Herbert Baker, it is 700ft long and faced with Portland stone.

The London & South Western Railway built the two railway bridges across the river to connect with Richmond. Barnes Bridge, a prime grandstand for the Boat Race, opened in 1849 but was widened and altered in 1895; the railway bridge at Strand-on-the-Green opened in 1869.

72. *High jinks at Kew Bridge, with the Star and Garter in the background. From a watercolour in the style of Thomas Rowlandson.*

ROADS

The two Roman roads that converged at Turnham Green (see p10) influenced the line of Chiswick High Road and the main route to the West. The High Road became a toll road in 1717 in a period when the care and maintenance of England's main roads, generally acknowledged to be diabolical, was farmed out to private enterprise. There were toll gates where Gunnersbury Station is now, at Kew Bridge and on the corner of Chiswick Lane. Later, a toll bar was put up across Devonshire Road to prevent carters diverting along Chiswick Mall to avoid paying the toll at Chiswick Lane. The turnpike gates were removed in 1872, when tolls were abolished.

The Brentford Turnpike Trust and its successors don't appear to have used the tolls they collected very effectively. In 1727 King George II and Queen Caroline spent a whole night journeying from Kew to London. A writer in the late eighteenth century complained that 'one might suppose from the state of the road between Hyde Park Corner and Brentford that there were no tolls to defray the expenses of mending the highway'; a coachman claimed the worst part of the road lay between Kew and Hammersmith.

As the 1815 map opposite shows, apart from the High Road, a few lanes linked Chiswick with Acton and a lane ran down to Kew Bridge. Other lanes connected the individual villages in the area – one running up from Strand-on-the-Green rejoiced in the name of Dead Donkey Lane.

In the 1820s the Duke of Devonshire constructed a carriageway to the northern entrance of his house, which became Duke's Avenue. Sutton Court Road running from Turnham Green to Burlington Lane was in place by 1846 and more roads were built in the building boom of the late nineteenth century.

After Chiswick Urban District Council purchased land from the Duke of Devonshire in 1923, the Great Chertsey Road (A316) was constructed and by 1933 traffic was able to cross the river on the new Chiswick Bridge.

The Great West Road from Chiswick to Bedfont was opened by King George V in 1925, and Chiswick Roundabout was built in 1936.

Between 1955 and 1957, Chiswick was effectively sliced in half by the construction of the Cromwell Road Extension (A4) linking Kensington to the Great West Road (it had been threatened for forty years). It was formed out of Hogarth Lane and suburban avenues. New roundabouts were built at the intersections with Devonshire Road and Sutton Court Road;

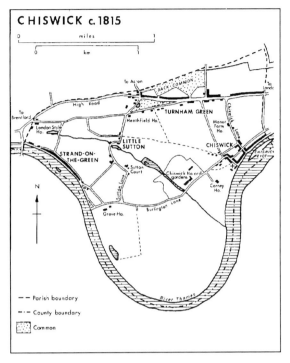

73. *Roads and lanes in Chiswick parish in the early nineteenth century. The routes out of the parish north ran along the lines of the present Gunnersbury Avenue, Acton Lane, Turnham Green Terrace. Wellesley Road is the road running south of the High Road. Lanes connected the four villages.*

75. *This toll house stood at the top of Chiswick Lane. It was discovered abandoned in a garden in Oxford Road in 1937.*

74. *Hammersmith toll gate, removed to Chiswick Lane about 1859.*

76. *Ceremonial procession along Chiswick High Road to mark the opening of the Great West Road in 1925. The Chiswick Empire is the building on the left.*

77. *Chiswick roundabout in 1957, before the construction of the Chiswick Flyover.*

78. *The Hogarth Flyover under construction in 1969. It was supposed to have been replaced by 1974, but is still there.*

79. *The first hole for the Cromwell Road extension being drilled in Harvard Lane on 24 October, 1955 by John Boyd Carpenter, Minister of Transport.*

some roads became cul-de-sacs and crossing points became pedestrian subways, first opened in 1956.

The Chiswick Flyover, the first major two-level highway scheme to be carried out in the Metropolitan area since World War II, was constructed in 1959, and in 1964 the A4 was linked to the M4 motorway by a two mile elevated section. At the time it was said to be the longest viaduct in Europe.

The seemingly precarious, one-way Hogarth flyover taking traffic from the Great Chertsey Road over the Hogarth roundabout opened on 17 September 1969. Traffic was light on the first day – which is hardly surprising since it was opened ahead of schedule with no announcement. It was put up as a temporary measure 'to remain in place for about five years when it will be replaced by a permanent structure'.

80. Looking south down Church Street in about 1952, before the construction of the Hogarth roundabout. The big building on the right is the Victorian Feathers public house; the tall structure in the centre is the old Lamb brewery, later the headquarters of the Standard Yeast Company. Drawing by T.A. Greeves.

HIGHWAYMEN

Until the nineteenth century, London ended at Hyde Park Corner and the roads out of town ran through unlit, desolate country – ideal territory for the footpads and highwaymen of the seventeenth and eighteenth centuries. The road to the west had a particularly bad reputation. It was the route to Windsor so the 'knights of the road' no doubt anticipated rich pickings from the king's important and wealthy visitors.

The dark, wild common of Turnham Green was a favourite haunt for robbers. In 1776 the Lord Mayor of London, driving in his coach with a large retinue of servants, was attacked and robbed at Turnham Green by a lone highwayman, who managed to escape. Isaac Atkinson was less fortunate. He was captured on Turnham Green after attempting to rob an old lady. The shrewd woman threw her purse over a hedge and, as Atkinson dismounted to retrieve it, his

stallion promptly made off after the lady's mare. He was executed at Tyburn in 1640 proclaiming 'there's nothing like a merry life and a short one'.

Legend has glamourised the highwayman as a polite and dashing figure, a gentleman 'turned to the bad', but your average highwayman was just a common or garden thug. Some *were* gentlemen – like William Page, who on Turnham Green responded to his victim's pleas by returning a gold wedding ring and five of the thirty shillings he had taken. Many were discharged soldiers; others, like Claude Duval, a famous west London highwayman, ex-servants. Dick Turpin, the most famous of all, was a butcher. Stories written after Turpin's death place him in Chiswick as well as in York but the real Turpin was an Essex man, hiding out in Epping Forest and, although highwaymen were very peripatetic, there is no evidence for him in Chiswick.

81. The Quicksilver Royal Mail coach outside the Star and Garter, Kew Bridge in 1835, with the bridge toll gate to the right. Painting by James Pollard.

On Wheels

HORSE DRAWN VEHICLES

There was no public transport on Britain's roads for many centuries. People either walked, rode or hitched a lift in a carrier's wagon. Stage coach services began operating in the late seventeenth century, but they were slow, uncomfortable and expensive – deterrents only reduced when the design of the vehicles improved and new road building techniques evolved. Travelling by stage coach reached its peak in the 1820s and 1830s before being knocked on the head by the railway.

Long-distance, gaily-painted stage coaches, like the *Courier* to Bristol and the *Defiance* to Exeter, would have been a familiar sight in Chiswick High Road, approaching the first staging post at Hounslow. In 1832, 22 stage coaches a day were running between London and Bristol alone.

People could also travel on the faster mail coaches – the first mail coach was tried out on the London-Bath road in 1784. The blast of the coachman's horn as the *Quicksilver* to Devonport approached the toll gate at Chiswick (mail coaches were exempt from paying tolls) must have caused a frisson of excitement – these coaches brought news as well as post.

Local coach services made two return journeys a day between Turnham Green and London in 1825 and by 1845 horse drawn buses left for London every quarter of an hour.

Horse drawn trams were operating to Young's Corner from Shepherds Bush, Hammersmith and Kew Bridge by 1882.

ELECTRIC AND MOTOR TRANSPORT

The first electrified tram service in London was inaugurated in Chiswick in 1901 from the headquarters of London United Tramways (now the Stamford Brook Bus Garage). Electricity for the trams was generated from a specially-built Power House on the south-east corner of the site. This enormous and elaborate structure, now a Grade II listed building, was designed by William Curtis Green and J. Clifton Robinson and put

82. *Horse-drawn bus from Turnham Green to the centre of London.*

up between 1899-1901. Two huge female figures, representing 'electricity' and 'locomotion' grace its facade.

Although largely superseded by Lots Road power station from about 1917, the Power House functioned as a sub-station until the closure of the trolley bus service. Trolley buses superseded trams in 1935 and survived until 1962.

The Power House is now home to recording studios, offices and flats.

Motor buses reached Chiswick in 1911. The Turnham Green bus depot opposite Gunnersbury Station, which closed its doors in 1976, remained virtually unchanged after its conversion from a horse to motor bus depot. Its proximity to the central overhaul works of the General Omnibus Company meant that it was often used as a testing ground for experimental and prototype buses.

The General Omnibus Company (later London Regional Transport) opened its large maintenance and engineering works off Chiswick High Road in 1921. It employed 2,000 workers and maintained 4,000 vehicles. In 1956 London Transport transferred vehicle maintenance to its Aldenham works near Elstree and the Chiswick works concentrated on engineering until its closure in 1988. The site has lain empty for the last seven years. There are proposals to redevelop it as a large business complex; whether or not these will go ahead has not been decided at the time of writing.

83. Horse-drawn trams at Young's Corner, about to turn into Chiswick High Road.

84. A battery-powered tram at Kew Bridge in 1883, one of many experiments before the tram service was electrified.

85. The Power House on the north side of Chiswick High Road, which generated electricity for trams and trolleybuses. It now houses recording studios, offices and flats.

86. *An elaborate wrought-iron staircase inside the Power House in Chiswick High Road.*

87. Employees leaving the General Omnibus Company's central overhaul works (opposite Gunnersbury Station) in 1937. This works (later the London Passenger Transport Works) provided many jobs in Chiswick between 1921 and 1956, when the maintenance division moved to Elstree. London Transport's engineering division closed in 1988.

RAILWAYS

The advent of the railways cut both journey times and fares by more than half – the journey from London to Bath was reduced from about 11 hours by coach to four and a half.

Chiswick's first railway, opened in 1849, was a branch of the London & South Western Railway Company's line from Richmond to Waterloo. Crossing the Thames by Barnes Bridge, it ran north-west through Chiswick to Brentford and Hounslow. Chiswick Station, designed by William Tite and opened that year, was called Chiswick and Grove Park in 1872, but reverted to plain Chiswick in 1920 (its first station master rejoiced in the name of Shadrach Clover).

In 1869 the LSWR opened a six-mile line from Richmond to Kensington. It crossed the river at Strand-on-the-Green and went through new stations at Brentford Road (renamed Gunnersbury in 1871 and replaced by a new building in 1966) and Turnham Green. This line also branched off at Gunnersbury to join the earlier line from Kew to Kensal Green and on to Broad Street.

The Metropolitan District Railway Company began running its own trains from the City to Richmond in 1877, using the LSWR line between Hammersmith and Richmond. The District constructed a new line from Turnham Green to Ealing in 1879 and added Acton Green Station (renamed Chiswick Park in 1910, replaced by a new station building in 1932). The District service was electrified in 1905 and Stamford Brook station built in 1910.

Until axed in the Beeching cuts of 1965, another railway line ran along the north and east of Chiswick from 1857. This was the North & South Western Junction Railway's branch line from Chiswick High Road to Acton Gatehouse Junction. At the latter station the single Chiswick carriage connected to the railway line from Kew, which took a circuitous route to the City. Designed primarily as a goods service, especially for coal from and to a coal depot by the station at Chiswick, it also carried passengers from

88. *The station and coal depot in Chiswick High Road (on the site of Ravensmede Way) from which the N&SWJR branch line to Acton ran until 1965.*

89. *District Line trains were pulled by steam engines until 1905.*

90. The old level crossing on Bath Road in 1933. The house on the right is 62 Bath Road, former home of the artist, Lucien Pisarro.

1858-1917, but not very economically. Oddly, this station in Chiswick High Road – where Ravensmede Way is now – was called Hammersmith Station until 1880, when it was renamed Hammersmith & Chiswick. In an attempt to attract more passengers, halts were added at Bath Road, Woodstock Road and Rugby Road in 1909.

There were level crossings on Woodstock Road and on the Bath Road. Residents complained about the length of time they had to wait at the gate in Bath Road: 'because the business of the goods yard at Chiswick has greatly increased of late years, everyone else's business must be interrupted', grumbled one. The level crossing at Woodstock Road had no gate, and exiled Russian revolutionary author, Sergius Michaelovitch Stepniak, was killed by a train here in 1895. Shortly afterwards a footbridge was put up.

91. Gunnersbury Station in 1963, the year before it was demolished to make way for the office block now occupied by BSI.

Local Affairs

PARISH AFFAIRS

Until the nineteenth century, affairs in Chiswick were administered by the two manors of Sutton and Chiswick, and by the church.

During the seventeenth and eighteenth centuries parish administration gradually superseded that provided by the old manors as successive governments, from the Poor Law Act of 1601 onwards, gave ever more responsibilities to the parish authorities. Out of the earlier meetings of vicar, churchwardens and leading citizens in the church vestry rooms, different kinds of vestries developed. Some until the nineteenth century were 'open' vestries, i.e. any ratepayer could attend and vote. This was a cumbersome arrangement as population increased, and many parishes opted to appoint, with government approval, 'Select' vestries, self-perpetuating bodies consisting of leading citizens, presided over by the incumbent of the parish. In 1836 Chiswick's Select Vestry consisted of twenty members, 'all substantial householders and ratepayers within the parish'.

The Vestry had the power to levy a church rate, collect the poor rate and make bye-laws. It was also responsible for administering common property such as the pound and wasteland. The main purpose of the church rate was to keep the church in good repair but it also paid for the expenses of churchwardens and officers such as the beadle and sexton, constable, pew-opener, organist etc.

The powers of the Vestry, however, were not very wide and it was difficult for it to undertake long-term projects. Its authority began to diminish when, in 1834, collection of the poor rate was placed in the hands of a separate Board of Guardians; and again in 1858 when the Chiswick Improvement Act was passed in Parliament. This Act was provoked by worries that the rapid expansion of London would engulf Chiswick and turn it into a slum. It appointed Improvement Commissioners who took over responsibility for roads, lighting, drainage and sanitation.

By 1875 Chiswick was governed by a Chiswick Local Board, replaced by the Chiswick Urban District Council after the passing of the Local Government Act in 1894. In 1927 the three Brentford wards were added to the six wards of Chiswick to form Brentford and Chiswick Urban District Council. This was incorporated into a Municipal Borough in 1932 with its own mayor and aldermen.

In 1965 the administration of London was completely altered by the London Government Act, and Chiswick was absorbed into the London Borough of Hounslow.

92. Chiswick Town Hall. The original Vestry Hall was altered and enlarged at a cost of £20,000 and reopened as the Town Hall in 1901.

Chiswick Town Hall. W 5787.

93. *Charter celebrations, 18 October 1932, the day Brentford and Chiswick became a municipal borough. This picture shows the mayors of Acton, Ealing and Barnes in the procession to the Town Hall (the carriage is turning into Bath Road from Stamford Brook Avenue).*

THE TOWN HALL

Until the nineteenth century the Vestry held its meetings in St Nicholas church, but the Improvement Commissioners (from 1858) met in a number of different premises, including the Roebuck pub, Chiswick Hall on Chiswick Mall (the former College House) and the Boys' National School at Turnham Green.

In 1874 the Vestry decided to build its own hall in Heathfield Terrace. This building, designed in 1876 by J. Trehearne, surveyor to the Chiswick Improvement Commissioners, cost £5,400. As well as local government offices it contained a large central hall and meeting rooms which were hired out for balls, concerts, lectures, auctions and classes.

In 1896 work began to enlarge the building (the Council used Sutton Court until the work was completed) and it was reopened as a Town Hall in 1901. After Chiswick was incorporated into the Borough of Hounslow the town hall was used mainly as a registry office, rates office and as a venue for classes.

LAW AND ORDER

England had no effective system of policing until Robert Peel's famous corps of blue coated 'bobbies' with their top hats and truncheons were introduced in London in 1829. Until then people shared collective responsibility for apprehending offenders, reinforced by the parish constable and in some areas, including Chiswick, the Watch and Ward system: Watch was the term for night duties of a special constable, Ward, daytime duties. If someone was trying to make an arrest it was obligatory for everyone else to join the 'hue' and to 'cry' out loud to attract the attention of others.

The inadequacies of this system led Chiswick to form its own association for the protection of persons and property in 1798. Subscribers paid an initial guinea and then at least 5s a year towards a fund which was used to advertise rewards and to defray the expense of prosecutions. By 1828 there were horse patrols along the High Road and foot patrols over a wider area.

In 1829, London's policing became centralised and by 1850 Chiswick had one sergeant and three constables. There was a police station in 1865 to the west of Windmill Place, and in 1871 a purpose-built police station (No. 210 Chiswick High Road, on the eastern corner of Windmill Road). It was manned by 73 policemen in 1890, 131 in 1926. The police moved to their present building in 1972.

Apart from the later police cells, Chiswick's only prison was the village lock-up or 'cage', put up in 1715, which stood on the north side of the High Road near Windmill Road. This would have been used for detaining drunks and law breakers before they were brought to trial.

Chiſwick Aſſociation,

For Proſecuting *Thieves* and *Felons*, &c.

WHEREAS Mr. *THOMAS DANCER*, of *Little Sutton*, a Member of this Society, hath lately been ROBBED of a large Quantity of

Purple Brocoli Plants,

And *ROBERT NICHOLS*, one of the Offenders, a labouring Gardener, who Works for Mrs. *HAMET*, near *Kew-Bridge*, hath been Convicted of Stealing the ſame, before *NICHOLAS BOND*, *Eſq*. and others, his Majeſty's Juſtices of the Peace, on MONDAY, the 19th Inſtant, at the Office, at *Kew-Bridge*; and the ſaid Mr. *DANCER*, is bound over to Proſecute one *WILLIAM SAUNDERS* for receiving the ſame, at the next Goal delivery for the County of *Middleſex*. And as *ROBERT SUMPTER* ſtands charged upon Oath of being concerned as an Accomplice with the ſaid convicted *ROBERT NICHOLS*, in the ſaid Theft, but hath abſconded and fled from Juſtice,---Now this Society promiſes to pay a REWARD of

FORTY SHILLINGS,

To any Perſon or Perſons who will Apprehend the ſaid *ROBERT SUMPTER*, or give Notice to the ſaid Mr. *DANCER*, ſo that he may be brought to Juſtice, to be paid on Conviction by me

JAMES ARMSTRONG,
TREASURER.

Auguſt 29, 1799.   *Turnham-Green.*

N. B. As a further REWARD, I promiſe to pay

Two Guineas,

On Conviction, as aforeſaid, to any Perſon or Perſons who will Apprehend or cauſe to be Apprehended, the ſaid *ROBERT SUMPTER*, he is upwards of 40 Years of Age, rather ſtout made, is well known in the Vicinity of *Old-Brentford*, did Work for me, and is ſuppoſed to be now at Harveſt Work.

94. Broadsheet advertising a reward to anyone apprehending the thieves of some purple broccoli plants, put out by the Chiswick Association in 1799.

FIRE FIGHTING

Buckets of water and manpower were the only way to fight fires until primitive fire engines were invented around 1600. Chiswick had a parish fire engine, kept in a shed west of the church, which was looked after by the beadle and staffed by volunteers.

The Great Fire of London of 1666 persuaded the more wealthy to insure themselves against fire risk. Their insurance policy was denoted by a 'fire mark', a metal plate attached to the front of the house showing the name of the insurance firm and the individual policy number – fire marks can still be seen on some older houses in Chiswick. The insurance companies organised their own fire brigades which, initially, attended fires only at the premises of the people they insured, but which later often vied with both the parish fire engine and each other to be first to quench the flames and receive a reward.

After the Vestry Hall was built, Chiswick's fire engine was housed there until the purpose-built fire station was opened in 1891 at 197-9 Chiswick High Road. The fire brigade had a new steam engine, a motorised fire escape and an ambulance by 1911 when it was claimed to be one of the best in London.

95. The old police station at the junction of Windmill Road and Chiswick High Road.

96. *The old fire station (197 Chiswick High Road). The long escape ladder was stored in the tower and the leather hoses dried there.*

The fire station also contained a mortuary where the firemen helped out to earn extra money.

By 1936 the fire station was no longer large enough for the (now full-time) fighting force of 18 paid firemen and their equipment. It was turned into the headquarters of the electricity utility and the fire brigade moved a few doors along to the corner of Linden Gardens where it adapted the premises of the recently-closed covered market building (see p.136), also using the Victorian Linden House as offices and flats for firemen. The brigade moved to its present site in Heathfield Gardens in 1963. The new fire station replaced Christchurch vicarage which was rebuilt in Wellesley Road.

WATER AND SEWAGE

Although water was piped to some large towns (not to individual houses but to standpipes in the streets) as early as the sixteenth century, most villages had to rely on springs and wells until at least the middle of the nineteenth century. Some wells are marked on the 1864 Ordnance Survey map of Chiswick.

Water was also sold by water carriers. A resident, reminiscing in the local paper about the 1870s, reports that drinking water was scarce in Chiswick: 'We had to buy it from a Mr Blizzard who sold it to us at 1/2d a pail. The water was obtained from the old artesian well in Hammersmith and was brought to the people of Chiswick in a huge barrel on a cart.'

However, residents didn't have long to wait before water pipes were laid in the area. Two companies supplied the water: the West Middlesex Water Works, with a pumping station at Hammersmith, and Grand Junction Waterworks from Kew. Nearly every house in Chiswick had piped water by 1897, and in 1903 the Metropolitan Water Board superseded the two private suppliers.

The Thames provided a convenient main drain for sewage until this was forbidden by the Thames Conservancy. Chiswick built its own sewage works in 1879 behind the present Edensor Gardens. These were altered and enlarged a few years later, and a pumping station built. They operated until 1936 when the West Middlesex Sewerage and Sewage Disposal Scheme was introduced and Chiswick's sewage was sent to the central works at Mogden, Isleworth.

GAS AND ELECTRICITY

By 1859 most of the parish was supplied with gas by the Brentford Gas Company. This company was taken over by the Gas Light & Coke Company in 1926 and superseded by North Thames Gas in 1963.

The Chiswick Local Board granted the tender to supply 'electric energy for private and public purposes' to Messrs Bourne and Grant in 1892, but before much was done they were taken over by the oddly named Aberystwyth & Chiswick Electrical Supply Company. This firm didn't proceed as 'expeditiously' as the Council expected and it was 1896 before it started laying cables. In 1914 the Council petitioned

97. The sewage works off Corney Road under construction in 1878.

98. The men who built the sewage works off Corney Road and the Improvement Commissioners who inspected the work. Behind them is a stationary steam engine.

99. Advertisement for the advantages of gas issued in the 1920s by the Gas Light & Coke Company.

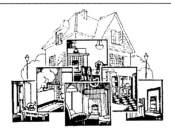

TAKE FULL ADVANTAGE OF YOUR GAS SUPPLY

Turn hours of toil into hours of leisure by using more gas.

With gas already laid on to your home the installation of additional gas appliances is a simple and inexpensive matter.

Gas is a supply of heat you cannot exhaust. It can easily be brought to any point in your home for any heating purpose to cook food, refrigerate food, boil water, warm rooms, heat the wash copper and iron.

And it demands none of your time and energy, needs no scuttles, flue-brushes or fire-irons. You just turn taps—

to take over the electrical supply but, after a stormy meeting, they were prevented from doing so by a poll of Chiswick residents, many of whom were worried about the potential cost, and who feared that the Council would subcontract electricity to the gas company, so creating a monopoly.

At the time, a correspondent in the local paper claimed that 'very many houses still have to adopt electric light, while practically all have still to benefit by the use of electric heating and cooking devices'.

Chiswick High Road was lit by gas from 1841. The Council's decision in 1904 not to switch the street lights to electricity was a disappointment. The local paper felt it particularly inappropriate for Chiswick High Road, the main road to the west: 'the road is brilliantly illuminated with the electric lights through Kensington and Hammersmith and it is only at Young's Corner, where Chiswick commences, that the gloom of dimly-lit ways begins'.

The Council finally took over the electricity supply in 1935, but it was not until 1939 that the transition of the street lights from gas to electricity was completed.

POST AND TELEPHONE

Chiswick Mall, Turnham Green, Strand-on-the-Green and Stamford Brook had post offices by the early nineteenth century, and Bedford Park and Grove Park when these estates were built (in 1903 telegrams could be sent from the two latter offices, but not received).

In 1894 the Turnham Green post office moved to 276 Chiswick High Road, then to 257 (the site of the Trustee Savings Bank) in 1913 and to the present building in 1966. Mail was sorted at 52 Clifton Gardens by 1896.

Chiswick residents didn't know their luck: in 1911 there were seven postal deliveries a day, mail posted before midnight was delivered to London and the suburbs first thing the following morning, and the Post Office was open from 8am to 10pm.

A telephone exchange was installed in the Post Office in 1903, but moved in 1913 to the building now named Autumn Rise in Sutton Court Road, and in 1954 to the present building behind the Post Office in Barley Mow Passage. The old exchange was used as a directory enquiries office until 1977.

100. Preserved Victorian pillar box at the junction of The Orchard and Bedford Road, Bedford Park.

101. The Post Office in Church Street, Old Chiswick.

A FREE LIBRARY

Chiswick's first public library opened in 1890 in the house on the corner of Duke Road with Bourne Place. Readers were allowed to borrow only one book at a time and there was no browsing round the bookshelves: books were selected from a catalogue and brought to the reader by the staff. It must have been hard work for the librarian and his one assistant since the library was open seven days a week and from 9am to 10pm every weekday except Wednesday.

Desperately cramped for space, the library moved to its present premises in Duke's Avenue in 1898. This was originally the home, built in 1882, of wallpaper manufacturer, Arthur Sanderson and his family, which Sanderson had generously given to the parish for use as a library: 'We thought it would be a fitting way of celebrating the Jubilee', he said in the letter making the offer in 1897.

The library was badly damaged by the fire at the nearby Sanderson's factory in 1928 (see p.89). It was repaired and a new extension added on the south side before reopening in 1931.

THE LOCAL PAPER

The *Acton Gazette*, which began publication in 1871, included news about Chiswick. It renamed itself the *Acton, Chiswick & Turnham Green Gazette* between 1888 and 1892; the *Acton & Chiswick Gazette*, 1892-1900.

The first edition of Chiswick's own local paper *The Chiswick Times* appeared in March 1895, price 1d. It was founded by Frederick Dimbleby (grandfather of broadcaster, Richard and great-grandfather of David, TV presenter and the present proprietor of the paper). 'Every care will be taken to make it a high class newspaper and there will be no pandering to the depraved tastes of the vicious' wrote Frederick Dimbleby in his introductory editorial.

Dimbleby also emphasised that it would not be a mere local edition of another paper, but a genuine Chiswick newspaper 'in which the interests of Chiswick will always have the first consideration'. The paper was renamed the *Brentford, and Chiswick Times* in April 1927 (after the merger of the two parishes) and is now the *Brentford, Chiswick and Isleworth Times*.

102. Chiswick Public Library, Duke's Avenue, in the 1920s, when it also contained a small museum.

Chiswick at Work

Agriculture and industries connected with the river provided the main employment in Chiswick in early centuries, but by 1801 more people worked as craft or trades people than in agriculture.

In the second half of the nineteenth century large firms like Thornycroft's shipyard, Sanderson's wallpaper factory and the Chiswick Soap Works also provided employment, supplemented by the bus overhaul works and the tram headquarters in the early twentieth century. Today the big industries have departed and their large premises converted to small offices or flats.

AGRICULTURE

In early centuries, crops such as wheat, oats and barley were grown, the latter said to be exceptionally fine in Chiswick. Cereal crops eventually gave way to fruit and vegetables as Chiswick and neighbouring parishes became 'the great garden of London' to satisfy the ever-increasing demand from the fast-growing capital. Market gardens and orchards covered most of the north west of the parish by 1746.

Cattle, sheep, geese, goats and pigs were kept – the latter illegally in the eighteenth century. In 1794, the surveyors responsible for Chiswick's roads reported that 'the hogs and swine are now grown very troublesome to the inhabitants of the parish as well as to persons travelling on the roads and much damage and mischief hath happened from them'. The surveyors were ordered to sell every hog and give the proceeds to the poor.

Twenty-three market gardeners or nurserymen were listed in 1826. The largest agricultural holding was Jessop's Grove Farm, just east of Grove House, with 310 acres covering most of the parish south west of Burlington Lane.

The nurseries included one at Turnham Green, near the later Thornton Road, and one at Strand-on-the-Green. That at Turnham Green was in place before 1740, and in 1785 belonged to Richard Williams, responsible for marketing the 'Williams pear'. By 1772, Strand-on-the-Green's nursery was owned by George Masters, who improved the Hotspur pea.

Many Chiswick residents will remember the nursery gardens of the Fromow family which closed in 1970. The Fromows established their business in 1829 at the corner of Wellesley Road and Sutton Lane where, in the 1890s, a magnificent glass conservatory and palm house was built. The Victorian building at the junction commemorates the Fromow name. In the 1930s, Fromows moved to Acton Lane – Sainsbury's car park covers the site.

103. Fuller's Griffin Brewery viewed from the river in 1890.

BREWING

For many centuries people brewed their own ale (ale, which was made from water, yeast and malt, became 'beer' when hops were added in the fifteenth century). There were at least five malthouses in Chiswick by 1736 and the large mansions had their own brewhouses.

In 1701 Thomas Mawson bought the brewhouse belonging to Bedford House, Chiswick Mall and what was to become Fuller's brewery, by Hogarth Roundabout, was born. It was sold to a family called Thompson in 1782 and in 1816 acquired its name, the Griffin Brewery – the name was unofficially purloined when another 'Griffin' brewery went bust.

The Thompsons ran into financial problems and raised more capital from one John Fuller in 1829. Control passed to his son John Bird Fuller, who recruited Henry Smith of Romford brewers, Ind & Smith, along with their head brewer, John Turner in 1846. The families of these three men have been running the company ever since.

Fuller's close rival was literally less than a stone's throw away. This was the Lamb brewery in Church Street, Old Chiswick. It was leased to John Sich and

104. *Unloading coal from barges at the draw dock, Chiswick Mall, about 1905.*

105. *John I. Thornycroft with his steam launch* Nautilus, Number One *boat from Messrs. Thornycroft's works at Church Wharf,* *Chiswick.*

William Thrale by 1790 and in the early nineteenth century the Griffin and the Lamb were said to be of comparable size. The Lamb brewery, still owned by the Sich family, was taken over by the Isleworth Brewery Company in 1929 and the brewery buildings used by the Standard Yeast Company until 1952, after which they were converted into offices.

FISHING

The Dean and Chapter of St Paul's, the owners of the Chiswick manors, also owned the fishing rights. A document dated 1181 shows that St Paul's charged 5s a year for the fishing, or every tenth fish caught. The Prior of Merton was granted the fishing rights and, in 1233, agreed to allow men of the manors of Sutton and Chiswick to use fish weirs in the river to catch barbel and lampreys at a rent of 23s a year.

Fishing provided a livelihood for a large number of families in Chiswick until the nineteenth century. The many species of fish that could be caught in the Thames included perch, gudgeon, barbel, smelt, salmon, eels and crayfish. But pollution from sewage and heavy industry then began to kill off the fish stocks and by 1829 23 fishermen and their families were receiving parish poor relief.

The riverside also provided employment on barges and lighters (barges without sail or motor power). Fourteen households of bargemen or lightermen are recorded in the 1851 Census. At low tide barges unloaded their produce, which included timber, coal, hops for the brewery, old ship's ropes for the Chiswick Press (see below), into horse drawn carts at Chiswick draw dock opposite Chiswick Lane. Goods loaded included the osiers cut on Chiswick Eyot from 1800. These were made into baskets for fish and market garden produce.

BOAT AND SHIP BUILDING

Boats and, later, barges were built in Old Chiswick and Strand-on-the-Green from at least the seventeenth century. In the 1880s and 1890s large electric launches were produced by Messrs Sargeant & Co's boatbuilding works at Strand-on-the-Green, including the *Viscountess of Bray*, then the largest electrically powered boat in the world.

Chiswick entered big-time shipbuilding in 1864 when Thornycroft's shipbuilding yard opened at Church Wharf, Chiswick Mall (on the site of Corney House, now the Regency Quay Development).

When he was only seventeen years old, budding engineer, John Isaac Thornycroft (1843-1928), built a 36ft long steam launch called *Nautilus* in his sculptor father's studio in Kensington. It caused a sensation on Boat Race day since it was the first steam launch able to keep up with the Oxford and Cambridge eights.

Thornycrofts specialised in high speed launches

106. The launch of the torpedo gunboat, HMS Speedy *in 1893 from Messrs Thornycroft's yard in Chiswick.*

and, later, torpedo boats and torpedo boat destroyers – Thornycroft's *HMS Lightning* was the first ever torpedo boat ordered by the British Admiralty. The difficulties of negotiating bridges downstream as the boats increased in size led to Thornycrofts move to Southampton in 1909. They were sadly missed: 'the stream of workmen passing through Chiswick in the early morning was a sight to see, but all is changed, and Chiswick streets are now fallen as quiet and mumchance compared with their former bustle, as Yorick's long-suffering headpiece', wrote one resident.

The house called Greenash (formerly Eyot Villa) on Chiswick Mall was built for John Thornycroft in 1882. A specially-constructed workshop in the garden housed his father, Thomas Thornycroft's, plaster-of-Paris original of the statue *Boadicea and her chariot* which now stands on Westminster Bridge. Later in his life, Thornycroft produced steam-powered vehicles and experimented with the new internal combustion engine.

During World War I, barges constructed of concrete, used to transport ammunition to France, were built at what became Cubitts Yacht Basin in Hartington Road – this was originally a lake in the grounds of Grove House. Shipbuilding was carried on here for a time after the War.

MOTOR CARS

Thornycroft's premises in Church Wharf were acquired by Gwynne's Engineering Company which produced aircraft engines under contract to the Admiralty there in World War I, and after 1920, the Albert and Gwynne-Albert motor cars. Gwynnes relocated to Hammersmith in 1930.

The car industry was also represented in Chiswick by H.J. Mulliner & Co, motor carriage builders of Bath Road (they occupied the old Bedford Park Stores, next to the Tabard Inn). From 1908 until 1968, Mulliners did coachwork for Rolls Royce and Bentley cars.

CHISWICK PRESS

A forerunner of the private printing presses, so much in vogue in the late nineteenth century, started on Chiswick Mall in 1809.

The founder of the Chiswick Press, Charles Whittingham (1790-1840), was an early exponent of recycling: he set up a paper mill to use a paper-making invention which involved removing tar from old ship's ropes and pulping the hemp to produce a paper with a strong, silky finish (the tar was used to produce printing ink). The first home of the Press was High House, where Orford House stands now, moving to College House in 1818 – the old building used

THE

LIFE AND ADVENTURES

OF

ROBINSON CRUSOE,

OF YORK, MARINER.

WITH AN ACCOUNT OF

HIS TRAVELS ROUND THREE PARTS OF THE GLOBE.

WRITTEN BY HIMSELF.

IN TWO VOLUMES.

VOL. I.

Printed at the Chiswick Press,

BY C. WHITTINGHAM;

FOR J. CARPENTER, OLD BOND STREET; J. BOOKER, NEW BOND
STREET; SHARPE AND HAILES, MUSEUM, PICCADILLY; AND
GALE, CURTIS, AND FENNER, PATERNOSTER ROW; LONDON.

1812.

107. Title page of Robinson Crusoe, *produced by the Chiswick Press in 1812.*

108. The devastated Sanderson's wallpaper factory after the fire in 1928.

by Westminster School on the eastern corner of Chiswick Lane South. The riverside location was chosen because of its proximity to the draw dock where barge loads of ships' ropes from London and other dockyards were unloaded.

The Chiswick Press specialised in producing high quality, small, dainty books that were easy to fit into a pocket. The presses were operated by hand and the printing was very fine, as were the woodcut illustrations. Whittingham's nephew, another Charles Whittingham, took over the business and in 1852 moved it to Chiswick Press's other office in Tooks Court off Chancery Lane.

The Whittinghams not only pioneered a movement towards finely produced volumes, but also to sensibly-sized books at reasonable prices. As such they posed a serious threat to booksellers of the time who favoured big books at big prices.

SANDERSON'S

Wallpaper manufacturer, Arthur Sanderson of Berners Street, W1, opened a factory in Chiswick in 1879 on the site of the former militia barracks (see p91). This factory, which was not much larger than a house and employed ten people, was sold and larger premises built on the south side of what is now Barley Mow Passage. This was expanded but by the end of the century, when the factory employed 250 and covered an acre of land, it was bursting at the seams.

Another, additional, building was erected on the other side of Barley Mow passage. The architect of this distinctive white-tiled building (completed 1902-3) was C.F.A. Voysey (who also designed some wallpapers for Sandersons). It was Voysey's only foray into industrial architecture and was described as 'a model factory', with a feeling of airiness and spaciousness. The building, now offices called Voysey House, has a Grade II listing

On 11 October 1928 a disastrous fire broke out in Sanderson's older building. It burned for several hours and the greater part of the premises, machinery and stock was reduced to a heap of ashes. For a week a mountain of smouldering paper 'glowed like a volcano', defying the efforts of the fire brigade, for whom it was the biggest fire they had ever attended.

Although Sanderson's at Chiswick were up and running again within three months once temporary floors had been put in, the fire caused terrible damage

109. *An early advertisement for Sanderson's wallpaper, which had its works in Barley Mow Passage, Turnham Green.*

Pier House Laundry
STRAND-ON-THE-GREEN
CHISWICK

A Well Organised Business.

FIRST-CLASS WORK.   GOOD COLOUR.

Telephones : **Chiswick 0378 & 1695.**

ON PARLE FRANCAIS.

Gentlemen should insist upon their Shirts and Collars being sent to us.

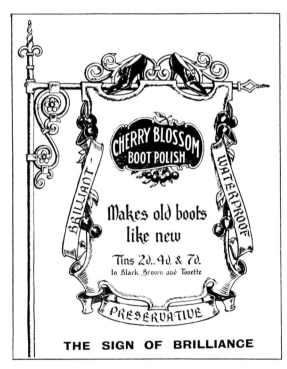

THE SIGN OF BRILLIANCE

to both the building and the business, and in 1930 Sanderson's moved to new and larger premises in Perivale. The old factory is now the Barley Mow Workspace see p138.

RECKITT & COLMAN

Probably the best-known product to be produced in Chiswick was Cherry Blossom boot polish, launched in 1906 at 1d a tin. It was invented by a chemist working for Dan and Charles Mason, two brothers who founded the Chiswick Soap Company in 1878 in Burlington Lane.

The polish was an instant success and by 1926 the firm had changed its name to the Chiswick Polish Company, manufacturing a whole range of shoe and household polishes, including Mansion House. The name was changed again in 1930 when Chiswick Polish amalgamated with the Nugget Polish Company to become Chiswick Products Ltd. Reckitt and Colman acquired the business in 1954 and new premises on the site by Hogarth roundabout were put up in 1967.

110. (Top left) Sanderson's factory building on the north side of Barley Mow Passage, designed by C.F.A. Voysey and completed 1902-3.

111. (Bottom left) Advertisement for Cherry Blossom boot polish, manufactured by the Chiswick Polish Company in Burlington Lane.

112. (Top right) The Pier House Laundry, Strand-on-the-Green, one of the largest laundries in London.

113. Windmill Road, looking south in the 1960s. The tall building on the right was the premises of the Standard Wallpaper Company until 1975. It was demolished in 1977 to make way for the office block formerly occupied by Wimpy International. Drawing by T.A. Greeves.

All production was transferred to Hull in 1974 and the building on the roundabout was demolished and replaced by the Hogarth Business Park. Reckitt and Colman moved their international headquarters back into the new complex in 1985.

The brothers Mason were renowned for their staff welfare. The Chiswick works had its own hospital with a nurse in attendance, a gymnasium, a sports ground, a model housing development for staff, and a club for female employees across the road in Boston House. Here, women up to a certain age were educated in the firm's time.

Dan Mason particularly, was one of Chiswick's great benefactors. He provided the recreation ground and pavilion near the Chertsey Road; the Chiswick Hospital and the Chiswick Memorial Club.

OTHER INDUSTRIES

Linoleum (made from oxidised linseed oil), is another Chiswick invention. Inventor, Frederick Walton, experimented with the product from a little factory on the west side of British Grove, and filed for a patent in 1863. In 1864 the business moved to Staines where it remained until 1973.

Pier House Laundry at Strand-on-the-Green was one of the largest laundries in London before its closure in 1973. It was started in 1860 by Camille Simon, a French immigrant. The brick facade of the main building in Thames Road, near Kew Bridge, still stands (it is now offices).

The very large red-brick block set back from Heathfield Terrace, between the Post Office and the town hall, was a furniture depository built for the Army and Navy Stores in 1871 (it is now flats). It was built on the site of a large barracks, the headquarters of the 3rd Royal Westminster Regiment at Turnham Green earlier in the century. One of the original militia buildings remains, rebuilt at the entrance to Devonhurst Place. The rest of the barrack buildings were demolished to make way for Sanderson's in the nineteenth century, and the Post Office in the 1960s.

In front of the old Army and Navy depository is a single storey building built in 1891, which has an interesting cantilevered roof made of wood. This building is known as the 'drill hall', although there is no evidence that it was used as such. It was an auction room for the Army and Navy Stores in 1892 and is an auction room today.

114. *The Old Pack Horse, Turnham Green in the nineteenth century. Horace Walpole used to bait his horses here on his way to Twickenham.*

Chiswick at Play

Little information is recorded on how people in Chiswick amused themselves before the nineteenth century. Apart from visiting the many pubs, they probably went to the twice-yearly fair in Brentford and took part in the public sports and celebrations held at various times of the year, particularly Whitsun. The profits from these events were used to swell the parish coffers.

By 1747, the Old Pack Horse pub on the corner of Acton Lane had an assembly room where balls and other entertainments were held. Fêtes took place in the gardens of the Royal Horticultural Society and mummers performed in shops and taverns around Christmas-time early in the nineteenth century.

The Chiswick Hall at 160 Chiswick High Road (now Old Cinema Antiques) was licensed for music and dancing in 1888. It also showed motion pictures from 1903. The Vestry Hall (now the Town Hall), built in 1876, became the centre for social life – balls, concerts, lectures and political meetings were held there.

A more serious pastime was to join the Armed Association – a sort of 'home guard' – formed in 1798, due to fears of a Napoleonic invasion from France. In 1803, under the same commander, this became Ye Old Chiswick Volunteer Infantry which pledged itself to 'march to any part of Great Britain for the defence therof, in case of actual invasion or the appearance of the enemy in force upon the coast.'

PUBS

Chiswick has never been short of pubs: 15 ale house keepers are recorded in 1716, increasing to 27 by 1759. One of the most famous was the King of Bohemia, named presumably after James I's son-in-law, the Elector Palatine and 'winter King of Bohemia'. It stood on the north side of the High Road opposite Chiswick Lane and is first mentioned in 1633. It ceased to be a pub in the eighteenth century when it was converted into three houses. The building was demolished in 1901.

Many official and unofficial meetings took place at

115. *The landlord greeting customers at the King of Bohemia. This early pub at the top of Chiswick Lane was converted into three houses in the eighteenth century. Italian patriot, Ugo Foscolo, lived in one of them.*

the 'sign of the Bohemia' and it was reputed to be the haunt of highwaymen. Its large cellars are also said to have been the hiding place of some of the conspirators who plotted to assassinate King William III in 1698. Sir George Barclay, a disaffected Scot, who wanted to restore James II to the throne, planned with forty others to waylay the king's coach in Turnham Green Lane (Wellesley Road) as he returned to Kensington from his weekly hunting expedition to Richmond Park. But someone called Pendergrass blew the whistle and the king put off his trip. Most of the conspirators were caught: Barclay, however, escaped abroad.

Travellers along the road to the west were well provided with inns. Pubs with the still-existing names of: the Old Pack Horse, Roebuck, Barley Mow and Coach & Horses were licensed by the mid eighteenth century and tickets for stage coaches could be booked at some of them in the 1820s.

The Old Pack Horse, on the corner of Chiswick High Road and Acton Lane, has a long history. 'Ye Pack Hors in Turnam Greene' is mentioned on a trader's token (used in lieu of money) of 1669. It takes its name from the packhorses which transported goods

before waggons were used and was apparently 'much respected' by travellers. The present building dates from 1910.

The Roebuck – to be renamed the Rat and Parrot in 1995 – was known for its extensive stabling and fine bowling green. The present stately, stuccoed building, with reliefs of stags on the pediments, dates from 1895.

In Old Chiswick there were once more pubs than there are today. Apart from the George and Devonshire and Mawson Arms/Fox & Hounds, which date to the eighteenth century, there was the Lamb Tap and the Burlington Arms in Church Street, and the Red Lion on Chiswick Mall; these have all been converted into houses. The Lamb Tap, now called Lamb House, ceased to be a pub in 1909; the Burlington Arms, now the Old Burlington, almost next door, in 1924.

Dating from the sixteenth century (an Elizabethan sixpence was found under the floorboards) the Old Burlington, with its overhanging upper storey and exposed timbers, is probably the oldest house in Chiswick. It was built initially as one house and later converted into tenements.

116. *The Old Burlington, Church Street, when it was an inn called the Burlington Arms. Next door was another pub, called the Lamb Tap (its sign can be seen on the left)*

The Red Lion, built about 1700 and licensed by 1722, ceased to be a pub in 1916 when it became Red Lion House. A large whetstone (now in the Gunnersbury Park Museum) used to hang outside the door, on which the osier cutters on Chiswick Eyot used to sharpen their tools.

The inscription on the whetstone reads "I am the old whetstone and have sharpned Tools on this spot above a thousand years." The last nought, though, appears to be a bit of graffiti added later.

Strand-on-the-Green is still famous for its old pubs. The Bull's Head was licensed by 1722, the Bell & Crown by 1751 and the City Barge by 1786 when it was called the Maypole Inn. The name was changed in 1807 in honour of the City barge moored nearby. The pub was destroyed by a bomb during World War II; the old bar, below the level of the footpath, is all that remains of the original inn.

THEATRES

Earlier this century there were two well-known theatres in Chiswick: the Chiswick Empire and the Q Theatre.

The Empire was opened in 1912 by Oswald Stoll, despite grumbles from local residents who felt it would lower the tone. The purpose-built theatre was a stately edifice, with seats for 4,000; the interior decor was pale cream and old gold with bottle green upholstery. It stood at 414 Chiswick High Road – its name is commemorated in Empire House, the office block erected on the site. Opened for music hall entertainment, it became one of the most prominent variety houses in the London suburbs, staging plays, revues and sometimes opera and ballet. Particularly popular was the annual pantomime.

Early performers were Little Tich, Gertie Gitana and Vesta Tilley. The Empire closed at the onset of the Second World War but reopened in 1941 when such stars as Laurel and Hardy, Vera Lynn and Arthur

117. *The Chiswick Empire, 414 Chiswick High Road. Built in 1912, it was damaged by fire the following year and closed for three months. The doors finally shut in 1959.*

118. *The Q Theatre where many famous names first appeared. It stood opposite Kew Bridge Station.*

Askey appeared. Terry Thomas, Dickie Valentine, Alma Cogan and Billy Cotton's Band performed there during the 1950s.

It died with dignity on 25 June 1959 when a lamé-jacketed Liberace played to a full house: 'A night of sadness at the Empire' was the headline in the *Brentford and Chiswick Times* the following day.

The Q Theatre (the name is a pun on Kew) stood opposite Kew Bridge Station on the site of what is now the office block of chemical engineers, Ralph M. Parsons. It was converted from the Prince's Hall which at various times had been a swimming pool, roller skating rink and finally a film studio.

The theatre was opened in 1924 by Jack and Beatrice de Leon. She was an aspiring actress who settled instead for a career in theatrical management, and he a solicitor who became a talented playwright and director. Due to the de Leons' astute management, the Q became one of the most important of London's small theatres, staging many plays that went on to become West End hits. The first works of aspiring playwrights such as Terence Rattigan and William Douglas Home were performed at the Q, and such luminaries as Vivien Leigh, Dirk Bogarde, Joan Collins, Anthony Quayle and Margaret Lockwood trod the boards here first.

In the 1950s the theatre fell on hard times: television was coming in, Jack de Leon died and the theatre needed major repairs. It closed in 1959.

There is still one professional theatre in Chiswick: the Tabard Theatre above the Tabard Inn, Bedford Park, which opened in 1985 as a 'theatre of new writing'.

119. The Palais cinema, 356 Chiswick High Road (the present site of Woolworth's). It opened in 1910 but closed four years later.

CINEMAS

Chiswick hasn't had a cinema of its own since the 1930s but there were at least three in 1913. The first purpose-built cinema was the Palais which opened in 1910 at 356 Chiswick High Road, where Woolworths is now, but closed in 1914. The Electric Theatre on the east corner of Duke Road and the High Road opened in 1910 and closed in 1933 when it was known as the Tatler. The Chiswick Hall at 160 Chiswick High Road was converted into the Cinema Royal in 1912. Known from its interior as 'the cave' it was prosecuted for overcrowding in 1914. It shut in 1933 and the premises now house Old Cinema Antiques.

CLUBS AND SOCIETIES

There were plenty of clubs and societies to join by the end of the nineteenth century: political clubs, religious clubs, working men's clubs and societies for activities such as amateur dramatics, music, angling, gardening and photography. Included in *Kelly's Directory* list of clubs and societies in 1899-1900 are the Turnham Green Scientific and Literary Society and the curiously named Cosy Club for Men at Furze Street, Chiswick.

Existing social clubs with their own premises are the Chiswick Memorial Club, Bourne Place which opened in 1919 as a club for ex-servicemen. Its premises, Afton House, were a gift from Dan Mason of the Chiswick Polish Company (see p.91). Chiswick Trades and Social Club (66-8 High Road) opened in 1921; Chiswick Club Society (13 Chiswick High Road) about 1903. The Studio Club in Woodstock Road (converted from two artists' studios), was formed as a bridge club in 1953 but soon abandoned cards for socialising.

SPORTS

The Oxford *v* Cambridge University Boat Race began in 1829 and was always a great day in Chiswick with throngs of visitors. Special (first class only) trains from Waterloo stopped on Barnes Bridge to give spectators a bird's eye view of the race. There were rowing clubs on the riverside from at least the nineteenth century and speed boats were raced on the Thames in the 1930s.

Turnham Green Cricket Club was formed in 1853. It was initially called the Turnham Green Devonshire Cricket Club in honour of its first president, the 8th Duke of Devonshire. There were many other clubs for cricket, tennis, bowls and football, cycling and rifle shooting. Ladies from Chiswick started the Chiswick Ladies Hockey Club in 1895.

The Duke's Meadows golf course, opening in 1995, is not Chiswick's first foray into golf. There was a golf club by 1892 on land adjoining Chiswick Station. The clubhouse was a converted farmhouse in what is now

120. Spectators at the Boat Race in 1871.

Staveley Road. By 1907 this course has been 'swamped with bricks and mortar' and ceased to exist. In 1930 a 'Tom Thumb' (miniature) golf course was opened behind the Chiswick Empire (414 High Road) – Tom Thumb courses were an American invention and this was the first one in London.

One of Chiswick's pride and joys was its much loved open air swimming pool. This opened in 1910 but closed in 1981. Protests and petitions continued for ten years until a new, but indoor, pool opened on the same site in 1991.

After the Chiswick UDC purchased land in the south of the parish from the Duke of Devonshire in 1923, many sports facilities were provided near the riverside. Large organisations like the Civil Service, the London Polytechnic and Prudential Assurance Company, as well as local firms, had their sportsgrounds here, and still do today.

The Council designated Duke's Meadows for public use and proudly built a tree-lined Riverside Promenade with a children's playground and a bandstand (a pergola of roses lined the road). Sadly, this 'lung for London' never became popular. 'What is wrong with the Riverside Promenade?', asked the local paper in 1958; 'it is Chiswick's bit of the river that is accessible to the public, but the public don't seem to want it.' No music has been performed in the bandstand for many years and the promenade now looks very forlorn.

121. Charity cricket match on Turnham Green, 1926. The Mayor of Hammersmith has just been bowled out.

122.   *Turnham Green Bicycle Club outside the gates of Chiswick House, Duke's Avenue in the early 1890s.*

123.   *Bathers at Chiswick Open Air Baths.*

The Royal Horticultural Society

The fêtes at the Horticultural Society's gardens in Chiswick were one of the main events of the London 'season'. In the 1840s and 50s, carriages going to Turnham Green lined the road from Hyde Park Corner.

The Horticultural Society (it didn't receive the Royal Charter until 1861) had been established in 1804 by a group of keen botanists and gardeners, including John Wedgwood (son of Josiah). Its aims were to improve horticultural practice by collecting and growing new species; determining the comparative values of existing species and disseminating information by shows, lectures and publications.

When the Society advertised for land for its experimental gardens, the best offer it received was 33 acres belonging to the Duke of Devonshire in Chiswick. This land was previously let out to market gardeners: Alwyn Avenue, Wavendon Avenue and Barrowgate Road now cover the site. It adjoined the grounds of Chiswick House and a private door was inserted in the wall between the two properties so that the Duke and his family could enter the grounds whenever they chose.

In 1821, the Society took over the land and laid out the gardens: half were allocated to fruit and vegetables; 13 acres to flowers and shrubs, and there was an eight-acre arboretum. Hot houses were built for the exotic plants brought back from China, Mexico and other far flung places and an artesian well was sunk to provide water for a canal to house aquatic species. In 1840 a huge and splendid conservatory was built.

To encourage good horticultural practice, the Society set up an annual exhibition with awards given to the best flowers, fruit and vegetables. The first 'public breakfast' was held in 1827 when tickets cost a guinea each. A long line of large marquees displayed the produce and provided refreshments; regimental bands entertained visitors throughout the day.

By the 1840s there were three fêtes a year in the Gardens. The May exhibition was considered the best for flowers; the July event the best for fruit, and the June show the best for company! A writer in the *Illustrated London News* in 1850 eulogised thus: 'The beauty of the ladies, the elegance of their costumes and the general appearance of gaiety that pervaded the scene, all combined to produce an effect which for a moment rendered it almost incredible that the busy haunts of London were so short a distance from the spot'. He liked the 'exotic orchids...peaches and pineapples' too.

In the late 1850s there was a move among the Fellows to change the emphasis from a showplace to an experimental garden, and in 1870 the Society reduced the acreage it leased to eleven acres. The glasshouses were demolished and the arboretum lost. By 1900 the Society was looking for new land for its gardens '...owing to the changes which are being brought about by rapid building operations, the neighbourhood of Chiswick is ceasing to be the ideal place it once was'. In 1903 the gardens were moved to Wisley.

As well as the shows, the Horticultural Society ran conferences and a training scheme for would-be gardeners. Joseph Paxton, designer of the Crystal Palace, was 'educated as a gardener' at Chiswick, where he caught the eye of the Duke of Devonshire who employed him as head gardener at Chatsworth House.

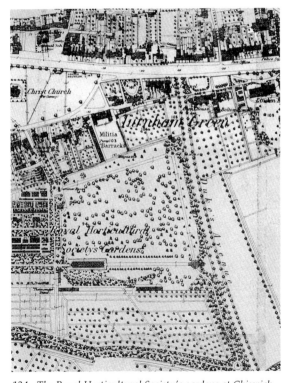

124. The Royal Horticultural Society's gardens at Chiswick, as shown on the 1864 Ordnance Survey map. They covered the area south of Heathfield Terrace to the present A4 between Dukes Avenue and Sutton Court Road.

125. *A fête in progress at the Horticultural Society Gardens, Chiswick in 1851.*

126. *The Great Conservatory in the Horticultural Soceiety Gardens. Built in 1840, it was 184ft long, 25ft high and 30ft wide.*

Chiswick at Prayer

ST NICHOLAS, OLD CHISWICK

There has been a church on this site since at least 1181 but, apart from the tower which was built in the fifteenth century, the church to be seen today dates only from 1882-4. St Nicholas served the whole of Chiswick parish until the first daughter church, Christchurch, was built in 1843.

Records show that the church was enlarged, repaired and altered many times over the centuries. An official inspection of the condition of churches in the diocese of London in 1252 describes the chancel as being in disrepair and badly roofed; in 1297 the chancel is noted as well built with windows well glazed and barred'; but, in 1458: 'the chancel suffers a defect in the lead roofing, so the rain drops within the chancel'.

The tower of Kentish ragstone was begun when William Bordall was vicar between 1416-35. The church that was there in 1785 was described as having a fine nave and a hammer-beam roof, but with 'free' pews (many people paid rent to sit in church) that were so narrow 'that it is impossible either to kneel, sit or stand in them but in discomfort'.

St Nicholas's parish registers survive from 1678. The marriage records of the eighteenth century suggest that Chiswick was a fashionable place to get wed – in many cases both bride and groom hailed from other parts of London.

Between 1882-4 St Nicholas was completely rebuilt in a Perpendicular style, designed by ecclesiastical architect, John L. Pearson. Due to the cramped space between the tower and Church Street, he designed the nave with a width almost equal to its length. Apart from a £1,000 donation from the Duke of Devonshire, all the rebuilding costs were paid by brewer, Henry Smith (the Smith of Fuller, Smith and Turner).

There were many burial vaults beneath the church but these were sealed with concrete before the new building was put up. The old monuments, though, were re-erected in the church. The most interesting is in the south chapel. It is an alabaster memorial to Sir Thomas Chaloner (d.1615) – see p.42 – and shows Sir Thomas and his wife kneeling over a prayer desk.

127. St Nicholas Church from the south in the eighteenth century.

128. The hammerbeam roof in St Nicholas church, built in the 15th century, but destroyed in 1863. It was hewn from carved walnut and described as one of the three best examples in England.

129. The tomb of Richard Wright, bricklayer to Lord Burlington, probably designed by William Kent.

THE CHURCHYARD

St Nicholas churchyard was Chiswick's only burial ground for many centuries. It was closed in 1854, although limited burials were allowed by special licence from the Home Secretary. For the next twenty years or so, people from Chiswick were interred in the large cemetery near Woking, run by the London Necropolis Company, but in 1870, the Duke of Devonshire gave the parish an acre of land adjoining the churchyard and more land was acquired later to form the present Burial Ground. Chiswick New Cemetery

on the corner of Staveley Road and Chertsey Road was consecrated in 1933.

It is difficult now to decipher the inscriptions of the many famous people (not all ex-residents of Chiswick) who are buried in the churchyard and Burial Ground. On the south side of the church is the tomb, topped by an urn, of William Hogarth, his wife, sister, mother-in-law and wife's cousin. Nearby are some fine table tombs, including those of actor, Charles Holland and Richard Wright, Lord Burlington's bricklayer. Burlington did him proud – the tomb is reputedly designed by architect William Kent.

Just to the west of the churchyard in the Burial Ground is a small mausoleum, designed by Sir John Soane, for landscape painter, P.J. Loutherbourg (d.1812), and the former tomb of Italian patriot Ugo Foscolo (d.1812), but Foscolo's remains were later removed to Italy. Some way down the Burial Ground, on the right hand side is the fine classical tomb of artist, J.M. Whistler (d.1903).

The Burial Ground is also the last resting place of Henry Joy, the trumpeter who sounded the 'Charge of the Light Brigade' (according to the inscription, although some historians claim he was actually the trumpeter of the *Heavy* Brigade).

ANGLICAN CHURCHES

By 1841, the population of Chiswick had climbed to 5,000, 3,000 of whom lived in Turnham Green. This was nearly a mile away from St Nicholas, Chiswick's parish church and the only place for public worship for those who couldn't make the journey, or couldn't afford the pew rents, was the Sunday evening service at the National Boys' School, Turnham Green.

Parishioners were thus understandably enthusiastic when the vicar of St Nicholas called a meeting in January 1841 to propose building another church. The money was raised by public subscription and the foundation stone laid in September 1841.

Christchurch, designed in the Early English style by Messrs Scott and Moffatt, was consecrated on 27 July 1843, its architect, George Gilbert Scott, later to design the Midland Grand Hotel at St Pancras. Christchurch was one of his earliest designs. It had no chancel – which both the architect and the parishioners deeply regretted. This was remedied in 1887.

Chiswick's other existing Anglican churches are: the stone gothic church of St Paul, Grove Park (1872); the red brick church of St Michael, Sutton Court, designed by W.D. Caroe and Passmore in 1909, which replaced a corrugated iron church on the Elmwood Road site and St Michael and All Angels, Bedford Park, designed by R. Norman Shaw in 1879, to cater for the residents of the newly-built estate of Bedford Park. St Alban's, Acton Green, in Acton parish was built 1887-8 (chancel and apse 1900), St Peter's, Southfield Road, in 1914.

130. *Christchurch on Turnham Green, looking north in the mid nineteenth century (artist unknown). The large building centre left of the picture is the Old Pack Horse pub on the corner of Acton Lane. The uniformed soldiers were probably stationed at the militia barracks in Heathfield Terrace.*

131. *The Methodist church, Sutton Court Road, built 1909 and replaced in 1988 by the present church.*

ROMAN CATHOLIC CHURCHES

In the 1820s Roman Catholics worshipped in a small chapel, described as a 'carpenter's workshop' in Windmill Place, Turnham Green, which also functioned as a school room. This became too small to accommodate the large numbers of Irish Catholics who arrived in the 1840s to work in Chiswick's market gardens and in 1864 a 'pretty little, red-tiled church, dedicated to St Mary, was built on the corner of Duke's Avenue and the High Road.

Ever-increasing congregations led to its demolition in 1885 and replacement with the present dignified, Italianate-style church dedicated to Our Lady of Grace and St Edward (the dedication to St Edward - Edward the Confessor - was added in 1903). The building was designed by a partnership called Kelly and Birchall. The tower, though included in the original plans, was not built until 1930, then put up as a memorial to those killed in the First World War and designed by Sir Giles Gilbert Scott, grandson of the architect of Christchurch.

After Our Lady of Grace was damaged by a bomb in the Second World War, a bungalow called Bolton Cottage in Bolton Road, Grove Park was used for mass and renamed St Joseph's. In 1954 St Joseph's became a separate parish and St Joseph's Roman Catholic chapel was built in 1959.

132.   The design for Our Lady of Grace and St Edward, *Duke's Avenue, published in* The Architect *1887.   The tower illustrated here is very different from the tower that was eventually built in 1930.*

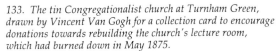
133.   The tin Congregationalist church at Turnham Green, drawn by Vincent Van Gogh for a collection card to encourage donations towards rebuilding the church's lecture room, which had burned down in May 1875.

OTHER CHURCHES

The modern building of Chiswick Methodist Church, Sutton Court Road, right by the A4, opened in 1988, replacing a large brick church of 1909.

In 1841 the Baptists and the Congregationalists shared a small chapel at the southern end of Chiswick Lane until the Congregationalists moved to Chiswick High Road in 1866. In 1883 the Baptists built an iron chapel in Annandale Road, replaced by the brick Chiswick Baptist Church which opened in 1897. Gunnersbury Baptist Church, Wellesley Road, opened in 1877.

Other churches have now gone: St James, Gunnersbury (where Blenheim House is now); St Mary Magdalene, Bennett Street, and Chiswick United Reform Church, on the site of the present 347-353 Chiswick High Road (just before Marlborough Road). Artist, Vincent Van Gogh, was associated with the tin church which preceded this stone church. He was accepted as a church worker here in 1876 when he was staying in Isleworth. He drew a picture of the Chiswick church for a collection card.

Places of Learning

A schoolroom at St Nicholas church, also used for vestry meetings, was repaired in 1642. In 1707 a charity school was built on the south side of the churchyard. The boys were moved to new premises in Horticultural Place, Turnham Green in 1813.

By 1819 the National Society for the Education of the Poor in the Principles of the Established Church had taken over most of the existing schools. In 1865 there was a National School for boys at Essex Place, Turnham Green, a National school for girls by the church, and other National schools at Horticultural Place and Thames Road, Strand-on-the-Green.

Additionally, there were two 'British' Schools – non denominational schools set up by the British and Foreign Schools Society – in British Grove from 1832-1864 and at Strand-on-the-Green in 1829.

Some National Schools became Board schools when Chiswick elected a School Board in 1872 as a consequence of the 1870 Education Act, which enabled authorities to pass bye-laws making education between the ages of five and 13 compulsory. The increase in Chiswick's population meant there was severe overcrowding between 1872-1887 and new schools were built in Glebe Street and Hogarth Road.

Education was reorganised by the Education Acts of 1903 – when Board schools became council schools – and 1944; old schools were closed and new ones opened. These are the state schools that survive today:

Now Chiswick's only secondary school, Chiswick Community School, Burlington Lane, opened for girls in 1916. Ten years later Chiswick County School for boys opened on an adjacent site. The two schools merged to become a co-educational grammar school in 1966 and, in 1968, amalgamated with the secondary modern schools in Staveley Road to become a comprehensive school.

Strand-on-the-Green junior, infants and nursery schools in Thames Road, started life as a British School and became a National school in 1874, when a new building was put up.

Hogarth primary and nursery schools, Duke Road opened in 1844 in the buildings now used by the Hogarth Youth and Community Centre and St Mary's Roman Catholic junior, infants and nursery school (which moved from Acton Lane in 1964). Hogarth Primary moved to its present premises at the bottom of Devonshire Road in 1958.

Belmont School, Belmont Road, opened in 1905 to replace the Turnham Green National schools;

134. The National School (demolished 1950) which stood on the south side of St Nicholas church.

135.   This British School was in British Grove between 1832-64, and is probably the reason why British Grove is so called.

Cavendish School, Edensor Road, opened in 1953 for juniors, infants and nursery children; Grove Park Junior and Infants school, Nightingale Close opened in 1952. Southfield School, Southfield Road, in the parish of Acton, opened in 1906.

PRIVATE SCHOOLS

There were many private schools in Chiswick during the eighteenth and nineteenth centuries. One of the most superior must have been Maurice Margarot's Academy at Turnham Green in 1780 'where young Noblemen and Gentlemen are Boarded and Trained'.

Several of the large mansions mentioned on previous pages served as premises for the private schools: College House, Walpole House, where Thackeray studied, Boston House, Sutton Court and Manor Farm House among them. A few of the big houses lining Chiswick High Road (see p26) also became educational establishments in their later life – Afton House, Belmont House, Bolton House.

Bedford Park residents opened their own rather avant garde school in 1884 (they formed a private limited company to do so). Classes, held in the School of Art, Bath Road, were mixed, lessons took place only in the mornings and there was no religious instruction since it was the view of the school's founders that belief in Bedford Park took many forms. However, the Bedford Park School proved too innovative for other residents who opened another, more conventional school – the Bedford Park High School at 9 Priory Road – a few months later. The schools co-existed until 1895 when they amalgamated.

ADULT EDUCATION

By 1869 adults could attend evening classes in the Chiswick National Schools, and both day and evening courses were held at the Chiswick School of Arts and Crafts, Bath Road between 1881-1899. The curriculum included drawing, metalwork, embroidery and other crafts. Modern languages, tapestry painting, plumbing, carpentry, enamelling, bookbinding and laundry work were added later.

The Middlesex County Council took over the School of Arts and Crafts in 1899, when it became the Acton and Chiswick Polytechnic. It was flattened by a bomb during the last war, rebuilt, but closed in 1982 when staff and courses transferred to Isleworth Polytechnic. The Arts Educational Schools have occupied the premises since 1986.

136. *Children of the former Beverley Road school in 1926, celebrating Empire Day.*

137. *Certificate of Merit awarded by Belmont School in 1919 'in lieu of a prize'.*

PEACE comes to the stricken land where the Soldier, the Worker, and the Peasant Boy, with Faith, Hope &
Love, Honour & Justice, have kept unsullied the Temple of Truth. Flowers spring up where PEACE has trod-
den. Beside her is Labour ready to carry out the work of Reconstruction, now that the Soldier's work is done.

138. Chiswick School of Arts and Crafts, Bath Road, designed by Maurice B. Adams in 1881. In 1899 it became the Acton and Chiswick Polytechnic but the building was destroyed by a bomb in World War II.

Caring for People

Before the seventeenth century the poor survived as best they could on scraps of food and handouts of dole money from religious establishments and more bountiful citizens. However, in Tudor times the 'sturdy band of beggars' increased alarmingly and society woke up to the fact that it had a duty to provide work for the unemployed and proper charity for those unable to work. This was enshrined in the Poor Law Act of 1601, which stated that paupers were to be maintained and set to work; the funds provided by a poor rate collected from every property owner in the parish. Vagrants from outside the parish – who were subjected to severe penalties ranging from whipping, losing their ears to hanging – were to be returned to the parish of their birth if they failed to find work within 40 days, or confined in a house of correction.

THE WORKHOUSE

An Act of 1722 encouraged parishes to build workhouses. One was built at Turnham Green in 1725. Chiswick's oldest resident in 1919, reminiscing about the past, claimed the workhouse 'was just where Gudgens the chemist is now'. This was 228 Chiswick High Road, now McDonalds.

Workhouses were intended as places in which work was provided for the poor. In Chiswick, amongst other tasks, female paupers were set to the manufacture of quills. Sometimes residents were employed outside the building and male paupers were employed sweeping and maintaining roads and draining ponds and ditches.

The census of 1801 shows that 105 people then lived in the Chiswick workhouse which was run by a Mr Goldthorp. Magistrates investigated the workhouse in 1807 following complaints that 'various Malpractices and Misdeeds have been committed'. They reported that the 'poor in the house are very turbulent and riotous', and 'that there is not any person either Master or Mistress in the said poor house, fit and proper to govern the poor, therein'.

Perhaps the Chiswick poor were too well fed: accounts show that they ate mutton, oxheads and beef as well as the staple diet of bread and cheese. Other intriguing articles of meat delivered to the workhouse were 'clods, stickings and mouse buttocks'.

In 1834, as a result of national legislation, several parishes in West Middlesex combined to form the Brentford Poor Union and workhouses were rationalised into larger units. The Chiswick poor were transferred to Isleworth (the workhouse is now incorporated into the West Middlesex Hospital) and the old building sold for £1,126.18s.

As well as the workhouse poor, there were the 'out of house' poor – people who were subsidised but lived in their own homes. After the establishment of the Brentford Union, all the poor in the various parishes received their stipend at exactly the same hour (Thursday at 11.30am) to prevent people claiming in more than one parish.

ALMSHOUSES

In 1629 a church house and other rooms in St Nicholas churchyard were used as lodgings for poor people chosen by the vestry.

Thatched almshouses at Strand-on-the-Green were built about 1658. These were replaced by new buildings in 1721-4. Extended and repaired in 1934 by money from the estate of Middlesex County Councillor, Hopkin Morris (and renamed the Hopkin Morris Homes of Rest), they were purchased and restored by Hounslow Council in 1974 and are still used for council tenants.

139. Old almshouses in Essex Place, Turnham Green, demolished 1886. Each of the four houses measured only 12ft by 9ft.

140. These almshouses on the bend of Sutton Lane were not pulled down until 1957.

141. *The almshouses at Strand-on-the-Green in about 1910.*

142. The War Memorial Homes, Burlington Lane, opened in 1922 as houses for disabled servicemen from World War I.

Almshouses had been built on the bend of Sutton Lane by 1676. They survived until the 1950s, and in the early nineteenth century tiny almshouses were put up in Essex Place, Turnham Green (demolished 1886). Almshouses in Edensor Road erected in the 1930s were replaced by Whittingham Court in 1976.

As a memorial to those who fell in the First World War, The War Memorial Homes for severely disabled ex-servicemen and their families were built on land donated by the Duke of Devonshire, off Burlington Lane in 1922.

CHISWICK MISSION

Spiritual solace as well as succour was provided by the Chiswick Mission from 1880 when Robert Thompson Smith began to organise meetings at a fruit and vegetable stall in the High Road. In 1890 the Mission purchased land from Alexander Fraser, Joseph Quick and George Reckitt (roads in the Glebe Estate are named after these men) and a Mission Hall was built in Fraser Street, which is now the premises of the Zoë Christian Fellowship.

The Mission provided breakfasts for thousands of impoverished children and dinners for hundreds of men, also such necessities as coal and coke. It was particularly busy after Thornycroft's boatbuilding business moved from Chiswick. Robert Thompson Smith also ran homes in Chiswick for motherless children – girls at the Roystons, Grove Park; boys in Burlington Lane.

HEALTH

By 1812 two surgeons were employed to look after the medical care of the poor, and in 1831 a Local Board of Health was appointed to watch over the health of the whole parish. There were the usual ills – TB, small-pox, scarlet fever, diptheria, para-typhoid, VD – but the main problem was cholera due to the untreated water supply. The medical board issued a set of rules for parishoners: houses were to be whitewashed, rooms ventilated and the people were to be scrupulous about clean water and personal habits.

Schoolchildren were subjected to regular inspections for cleanliness by the Medical Inspector. In 1920 he reported that '13 girls were classed as dirty while 111 were fairly clean. Among the boys, 22 were dirty and 118 only fairly clean'.

A public wash house, containing slipper baths, spray baths and a communal laundry opened in 1924 in Essex Road, Turnham Green (it closed in the 1970s).

The country's population was not very long-lived. Out of the 31,377 people living in Chiswick parish in 1903 there were only 67 persons aged over 65 and only one over 90.

HOSPITALS

For many years, Chiswick's Medical Officer pleaded for a separate isolation hospital for infectious diseases. In 1904 this was opened in Clayponds Road, Brentford to serve both Brentford and Chiswick (it became a maternity hospital in 1925).

Vol. I. No. 2. FEBRUARY 1937

The Home Messenger.

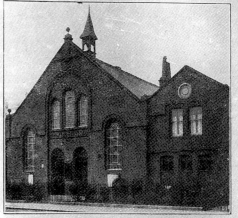

A MAGAZINE FOR THE PEOPLE.

Chiswick Mission.
" BRANCH OF THE SHAFTESBURY SOCIETY AND RAGGED SCHOOL UNION."

President—MR. R. T. SMITH

Vice-Presidents—Sydney Powell, Esq.
Mr. J. P. Nicholls. Mr. A. A. Allwright,
Councillor W. H. Cato, Dr. Montague Teuten.

Treasurer—MR. J. GURNEY

Superintendent and Secretary—
MR. F. H. GROGAN,
67, Glebe Street, Chiswick, W. 4.

HOMES FOR THE AGED,
43 ANNANDALE RD., CHISWICK.
11 QUICK ROAD, CHISWICK.

Auditors—
MESSRS. J. & A. W. SULLY & Co.,
Chartered Accountants,
19 & 21 Queen Victoria Street, E.C.

Bankers—
Westminster Bank, Ltd.

CHISWICK MISSION, Fraser Street, Chiswick.
(Supported by Voluntary Contributions).

SERVICES ON THE LORD'S DAY.
Morning at 11. Evening at 6.30.

3.0 p.m. Lads' Bible Class
3.0 p.m. Young Women's Bible Class

SUNDAY SCHOOL
Morning at 10 o'clock. Afternoon at 3 o'clock.

Monday	3.0	Women's Own Sisterhood
"	5.0	Penny Bank
"	6.30	Girls' Life Brigade
Tuesday	3.0	B.W.T.A.
"	8.0	Christian Endeavour Society
Wednesday	8.0	Boys' Club.
"	8.0	Service
Thursday	6.30	Band of Hope
"	7.30	Cripples' Guild
"	8.30	Choir Practice
Friday	6.30	Girls' Life Brigade
Saturday	8.0	Prayer Meeting

ALL SEATS FREE.

Taylor & Read, 31 Churchfield Road, Acton, W. 3.

Annual Subscription 2/6 by Post
Monthly 2d.

143. *Title page of a magazine produced by the Chiswick Mission, showing the mission building in Fraser Street.*

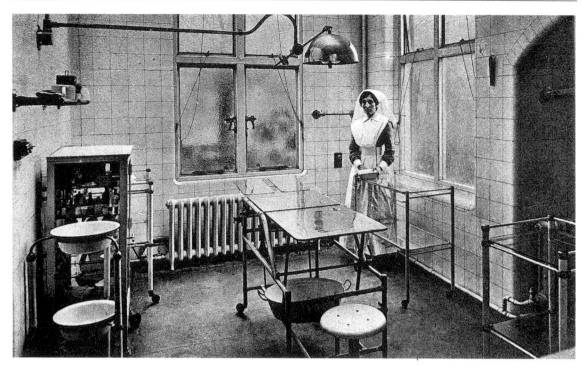

144. The operating theatre of St Joseph's Hospital, attached to St Mary's convent in Burlington Lane. Florence Nightingale was involved with the design of the Hospital.

Chiswick had a cottage hospital by 1911. Endowed by Daniel Mason of Chiswick Products, it opened in two cottages in Burlington Lane, but a year later moved to new premises in Rothbury House, Chiswick Mall, with accommodation for 32 patients – ten men, eight women and 14 children. This building was replaced in 1936. In 1943 it became a maternity hospital and in 1986 a home for the elderly, called Chiswick Lodge.

Another hospital was St Joseph's, Burlington Lane, which cared for poor and incurable women and girls. It was attached to St Mary's Convent run by the Anglican Order of St Mary and St John, which was founded in Kensington in 1868. In 1896 the Order acquired land in Chiswick from the Duke of Devonshire and built the premises now known as St Mary's Convent and Nursing Home. The architect was Charles Ford Whitcombe and Florence Nightingale was consulted about the design of the hospital. The nursing home and operating theatre opened in 1912. St Mary's now cares for old and handicapped women.

The mentally ill were sent to an asylum at Hoxton until the Hanwell asylum opened in 1831. A private mental hospital in Chiswick, with more humane ideas on how to look after the mentally sick, was run by a family of doctors called Tuke for nearly a hundred years. From 1837 to 1892 its premises were Manor Farm House, Chiswick Lane. It then moved to Chiswick House where it remained until 1929.

CHISWICK WOMEN'S AID

Britain's first official refuge for battered women was opened in Chiswick in 1971, although its origins were a band of women protesting about shop prices in the High Road. Rallying support for their cause they discovered how isolated many young mothers felt, cut off in their own houses. This led Erin Pizzey to persuade the Council to allow a derelict house (2 Belmont Terrace) to be used as a community centre – somewhere women could meet and escape to for a while.

However, some women (those suffering violence) had nowhere else to go. As word of Erin Pizzey's work for battered women spread, the centre was inundated with pleas for help from all over the country It moved to larger premises in Chiswick High Road and filled up as soon as the doors opened. Chiswick Women's Aid became Chiswick Family Rescue in 1980 and changed its name to Refuge in 1993.

The Building Boom

The Census of 1801 lists 3,235 inhabitants in the parish of Chiswick, when there were 589 houses. A hundred years later the population had soared to 28,513 living in 5,308 homes (these figures exclude that part of the area which lies in the parish of Acton).

During the nineteenth century London began to spread its tentacles further and further outwards; the arrival of the railways also made it easier for those who worked in the capital to return in the evenings to the delights of the countryside.

Chiswick's transition from village to suburb began to speed up after 1871 when the first new middle class housing developments were completed. The population, which had been rising fairly steadily, almost doubled between 1871 and 1881 and continued rising until the 1930s.

Some of the development was piecemeal, building on the sites of demolished properties or on vacant plots along existing roads, but there were other, larger developments where new housing estates were laid out along new roads.

More houses were built in the already established residential centres of Chiswick Mall, Strand-on-the-Green and along Chiswick High Road. By the middle of the twentieth century the separate villages had been joined up, the open areas replaced with bricks and mortar.

HOMES FOR LOCAL WORKERS

New homes were needed for the workers in Chiswick's market gardens, breweries and other trades, and the first sizeable housing development was Chiswick New Town. By 1838 seven streets of terraced houses had been built on former market gardens north of Hogarth Lane, west of Chiswick Field Lane (now Devonshire Road). The chapel of St Mary Magdalene was added in 1848.

Contemporary accounts suggest the houses were squalid. They fronted directly onto the roads which were not made up until the 1880s, and the occupants were poor: half the paupers in the parish came from Chiswick New Town in 1851. Richer residents deplored this development 'which attracted, well, not the same class of person', said one. Chiswick New Town was demolished in the 1950s and replaced by council flats

Starting in about 1869 another planned development of working-class homes was laid out between Chiswick New Town and the High Road, bounded by Duke Road on the west and Devonshire Road on the east. Called the Glebe Estate because it was built on glebe land (a field belonging to the vicar), it was always a bit posher than Chiswick New Town, and today, when it has come up in the world, is described as 'Chiswick's Little Chelsea'.

The mainly terraced houses were tightly packed together and almost all were rented rather than pur-

145. Dale Street on the Glebe Estate, developed n the 1870s/1880s. At first glance the houses seem identical but there are, in fact, many different designs.

146. Old hay loft and stables on the Glebe Estate where local shop owners kept their horses and carts.

chased. Few had any back access and coal was kept under the stairs. A self-contained little enclave, the Glebe Estate had its own pub, the Bolton, a Mission Hall, a school and shops on almost every corner.

The land between Devonshire Road and Chiswick Lane was developed as working-class homes between 1891 and 1901. Known as the ABC estate because of the alphabetical arrangement of its roads – Ashbourne Grove, Balfern Grove, Cornwall Grove etc – the houses were larger than those on the Glebe Estate but each house was intended as two tenements.

Development of the area around what is now

Chiswick Park station started in the 1880s. These were modest houses and probably largely tenanted by workers in the laundries of Acton – there were over 170 laundries in Acton in 1890.

A development of slightly more superior homes, which were purchased rather than rented, was built near the river (Riverview Grove and surrounding roads) from 1904.

HOMES FOR COMMUTERS

Of the housing developments intended for the middle and upper echelons, built primarily to take advantage of the new railway stations, the two best known are Bedford Park and the Grove Park Estate, both dealt with later. But these are by no means Chiswick's only prestigious housing developments.

Adam Askew, who owned land running south from the High Road in the west of the parish was quick to take advantage of the new railway line – he was developing his estate in and around Oxford and Cambridge Roads while the tracks were being laid in the 1860s. One hundred and seventy four houses had been built by 1914. Some were very grand but Askew built a wide range of different houses, a parish hall (associated with the church of St James – now gone) and a pub (the Pilot in Wellesley Road).

The Homefield Estate, between the High Road and Homefield Recreation Ground, was begun in the 1890s

147. Large villas in Wellesley Road, built in the 1870s. Drawing by T.A. Greeves.

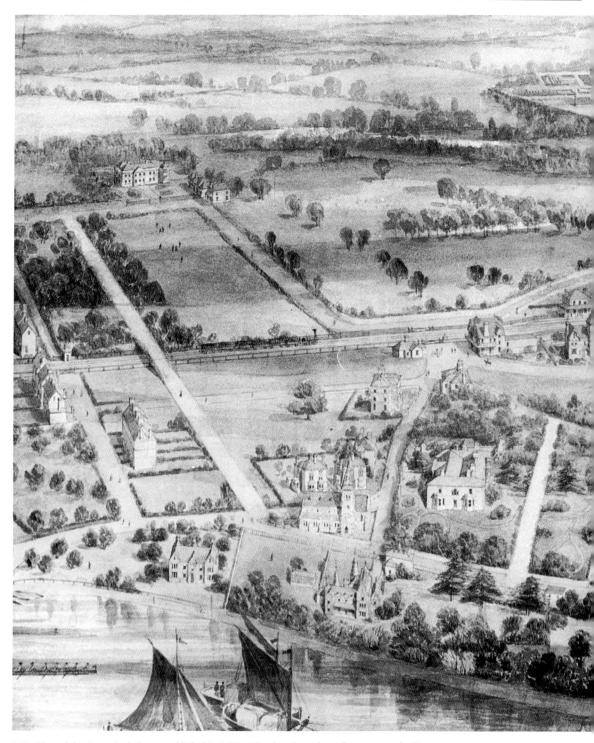

148. Plan of the Grove Park Estate published in 1867. The church on the right was never built.

149. Grove End, built in 1861 by John Pulman, a chamois leather merchant, for his own occupation.

but not completed until after the First World War.

Barrowgate Road was laid out in 1882 and twenty large houses built. A massive mansion, called Devonhurst, was put up in Duke's Avenue, and another, Watchfield, on the other side of Sutton Court Road. After the Royal Horticultural Society's removal to Wisley and the demolition of Devonhurst, new roads and middle class housing were built on the site in the early 1900s.

Starting in the last decade of the nineteenth century, road after road of neat villas were laid out for the middle classes. Good examples are in the area around Fauconberg Road and west of Bedford Park. Large blocks of flats, most described as 'mansions', were built as well – 11 blocks had been completed by 1914.

After 1911 the rate of building slowed down – between then and 1950 it was half that of the previous 40 years. By 1921 the population of Chiswick parish numbered 40,938.

GROVE PARK ESTATE

In 1847 The Duke of Devonshire owned a staggering 50% of the land in Chiswick parish. The new Chiswick railway station of 1849 and the railway tracks were on his land and in 1867 he publicised plans for a spacious estate between the river and the railway and built the Grove Park Hotel to attract visitors to the riverside.

However, it was 1871 before any housing was put up on the Grove Park Estate, bounded on the west by Grove Park Gardens and Cavendish Road on the east.

There were already two grand houses in the area –

Grove House (p31) and Grove End, 'a fantastic redbrick structure with tall capped towers', built in 1861 (the art deco block of flats, Hartington Court, put up in 1938, replaced it). These two large houses were left standing to raise the tone of what the Duke intended to be a prestigious estate combining huge mansions for rich merchants with houses designed to appeal to the less wealthy middle classes.

There was a church, St Paul's, built by the Duke, a pub, the Grove Park Hotel, and many facilities for the sporty: boathouses on the river, a putting green, a tennis club, cricket, golf as well as punting on the lake in the grounds of Grove House. There was also a Grove Park Society

When Grove House was demolished in 1928, houses and flats were put up on its site (Kinnaird Avenue and surrounding roads). Apart from the large gothic houses on the riverfront near Strand-on-the-Green, which were built in the 1870s, the other sizeable developments along the river came later: Thames Village (1956), Chiswick Staithe (1965), Chiswick Quay (1975).

The houses in Chiswick Quay, each with its own mooring, were built around the old lake of Grove House, which was commandeered for barge building in World War I. In the 1920s the lake had turned into a floating village of houseboats. An idyllic place to live, according to one inhabitant: 'perfect peace and quiet, wildfowl and only twenty minutes from Waterloo Station. But of course we are all mad'. However, the boat owners were booted out in 1969, though they resisted to the extent of calling in the Ombudsman.

150. *No. 61 Hartington Road, the home of Eamonn Andrews in 1965.*

151. *Hartington Court, Hartington Road, art deco flats built in 1938 on the site of Grove End.*

The First Garden Suburb

'Bedford Park, Chiswick W. The healthiest place in the world (annual death rate under 6 per thousand)' ran the advertisement for this new estate in 1883. Bedford Park was only one of many later nineteenth century housing developments in Chiswick, but it became famous for its architecture and its association with the aesthetic movement which stood for a revolt against Victorian materialism, vulgarity and ostentation and a move towards simplicity and appreciation of beauty in everyday life – ideals promoted by people such as John Ruskin and William Morris. The informal leafy layout of Bedford Park was also the prototype for later garden suburbs like Hampstead and Letchworth.

Bedford Park was developed by Jonathan Carr (1845-1915), a cloth-merchant and property speculator, who moved in literary and artistic circles. Identifying a need amongst the cultured middle class for suitable and affordable homes close to London, he planned a new kind of estate of aesthetically acceptable houses at cheap rents set in an informal layout with plenty of greenery.

DEVELOPING THE ESTATE

The choice of location was determined by family ties and the proximity of Turnham Green railway station, built in 1869. Carr's father-in-law, Hamilton Fulton, lived in Bedford House, which was designed in the late eighteenth century by one John Bedford, and is not to be confused with Bedford House on Chiswick Mall. Bedford House was one of three Georgian houses that stood north of Acton Green – Sydney House, demolished 1906 and replaced by flats, and Melbourne House were the others. The grounds of Bedford House contained an arboretum planted by horticulturist and botanist, Dr John Lindley, who lived in the house between 1834 and 1865 and who had been secretary of the Royal Horticultural Society between 1858 and 1863. It was the mature trees from this arboretum and from the surrounding orchards and fields which Carr was to preserve.

In 1875 Carr purchased 24 acres of his father-in-law's grounds which lay in Acton parish and more land was acquired rapidly in Acton, Ealing and Chiswick. The eventual area for the estate was 113 acres, stretching north-south from Southfield Road to Acton Green, and Abinger Road to Rusthall Avenue, east-west. Carr's original intention, announced in *Building News* 1877, was to build 900 houses in five years. In the event, he built about 500 in nine years on

152. The Georgian Bedford House, before the front was obscured by the parade of shops built in 1924.

half the land acquired. In 1881, with the core of Bedford Park complete, he was planning new property ventures elsewhere. To raise capital for these he formed a company, Bedford Park Limited, but this collapsed with huge liabilities five years later. The land was sold off piecemeal and developed in various architectural styles, without any of the controls exercised by Carr.

After the First World War, the character and architectural merit of Bedford Park went unrecognised: houses became dilapidated and were converted into flats. A few were demolished – notably Tower House, the grandest of all the Bedford Park houses, where Jonathan Carr had once lived as 'Lord of the Manor' before being obliged to move to a smaller house on the estate because of the failure of his property speculations. St Catherine's Court was put up on the site of Tower House in the 1930s.

When Acton Council erected a block of flats, built of unsympathetic yellow brick, on the corner of Marlborough Crescent and Bedford Road, architect and local resident Tom Greeves and retired builder Harry Taylor, decided the time had come to safeguard the area. In 1963 they formed the Bedford Park Society with poet John Betjeman as patron. Following a four-year campaign by the Society the Ministry of Housing gave a statutory Grade II listing to 356 houses in Bedford Park in 1967 (not every house is listed). Ealing and Hounslow councils declared their respective sections of Bedford Park conservation areas in 1969/70. Bedford Park holds its own two-week festival each summer.

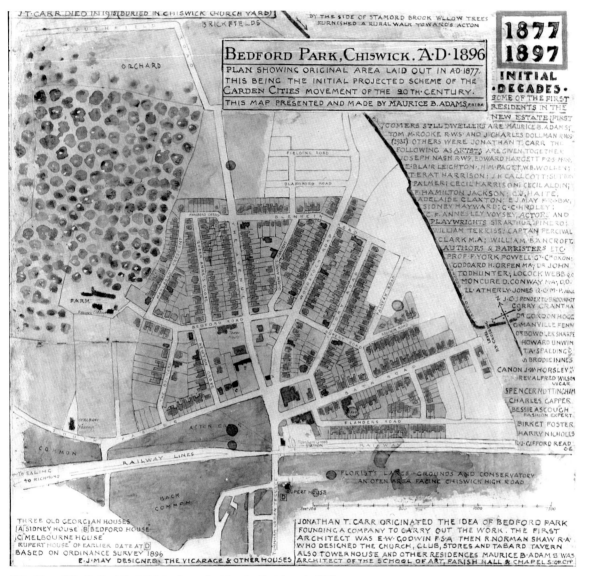

153. Plan of the Bedford Park Estate, drawn by Maurice B. Adams in 1931.

THE ARCHITECTS

From the outset, Carr commissioned well known architects to build his simple villas and public buildings. As a reaction to the vogue for stucco-clad houses, they elected to build in red brick, with tile hanging and lots of white painted woodwork. The style is known as Queen Anne revival but actually derives from rural English architecture of the seventeenth century with elements of Dutch and Flemish architecture thrown in.

Carr's first architect was E.W. Godwin, who produced two designs, but their association foundered

and Carr next commissioned designs from the more distinguished, R.Norman Shaw, the designer of the old New Scotland Yard building on Victoria Embankment. Shaw was the estate architect from 1877 to about 1880 and was succeeded by his assistant E.J. May, who lived in Bedford Park. Other architects involved were the firm of Coe and Robinson, William Wilson and Maurice B.Adams, also a Bedford Park resident.

One of the attractions of the estate was the presence in many houses of purpose-built studios for artists.

BEDFORD PARK, CHISWICK, W. | Close to TURNHAM GREEN STATION. Trains every few minutes.

THE HEALTHIEST PLACE IN THE WORLD | The Estate is built on gravelly Soil and has the most approved Sanitary arrangements.

(Annual Death Rate under 6 per Thousand).

About 500 Houses on the Estate, all in the picturesque Queen Anne style of Architecture.

A Garden and a Bath Room with Hot and Cold water to every house, whatever its size.
A Kindergarten and good Cheap Day Schools on the Estate, and a School of Art.
Also Church, Club (for Ladies & Gentlemen), Stores, "The Tabard Inn," Tennis Courts, &c.
Several houses now to let at rents varying from £30 to £130.

154. An advertisement for the Bedford Park Estate in 1883.

Another was the lack of basements – servants shouldn't be obliged to work underground, claimed reformists of the time – but this might have been more a practical consideration since the Stamford Brook, which ran along the eastern edge of the estate, made the area wet and prone to flooding.

In the 1880s you could rent what was advertised as a three bedroom house (although it also contained three attic rooms) with two sitting rooms for £32 a year; a seven-bedroom detached house with three sitting rooms for between £85-£90 pa. The railway fare from Turnham Green to Victoria cost 11d, 8d or 5½d, depending on whether you travelled first, second or third class.

THE COMMUNITY

Shaw designed the public buildings intended to give Bedford Park the air of a self-contained community: the Bedford Park Club in 1878 (now the London Buddhist Vihara); the block in Bath Road (1880) containing the Tabard Inn, which has wall tiles by William de Morgan and Walter Crane, and the Stores (now offices), Bedford Park's own superstore with a post and telegraph office and its own livery stable.

Shaw was also responsible for St Michael's church (1879), although Maurice Adams had a hand in this design, and it was Adams who designed Bedford Park's School of Art in 1881. This was destroyed during World War II and the Arts Educational Schools are now on the site.

155. *Poster drawn by Maurice B. Adams in collaboration with R. Norman Shaw in 1877 showing the different types of houses available.*

156. *View of Bedford Park from Newton Grove, 1882. The large house in the centre of the picture is the Tower House, designed by R. Norman Shaw for Jonathan Carr.*

157. View from South Parade across Acton Green looking towards St Michael and All Angels, 1882. The parish hall is not shown since it wasn't built until 1887. On the right is the Tabard Inn and the Stores.

Bedford Park also had its own schools (see p108), voluntary fire brigade and a Vigilance Committee which negotiated matters with the local councils.

A lively little community with an air of 'cozy comfort' grew up in Bedford Park. For the year 1883-4 it had its own magazine *The Bedford Park Gazette*. Social life centred on the club. There were dances every month, masquerades, a theatre (in which Ronald Colman first trod the boards), a natural history society, a musical society and a Ladies' Discussion Society. Regular lectures were held on scientific, literary and political subjects.

Long-time resident, Sybil Pearce, remembers the club as being rather like an old country house with big coal fires, large leather sofas, soft shaded lamps and a 'delicious smell of beeswax'. Plays in the theatre were contributed by local writers and played to packed houses for a week at a time. Associated with the club was the tennis club, with courts in the garden of Tower House.

Although not a commercial success, Bedford Park attracted considerable attention, not just for its aesthetic roots and novel architecture, but also because of its free-thinking, rather Bohemian inhabitants, who were said to go around in carpet slippers and be partial to fancy dress balls.

Some people found it pretentious. A satire called *The Ballad of Bedford Park* appeared in the *St James's Gazette* in 1881. The last two verses read:

"Now he who loves aesthetic cheer
    and does not mind the damp
May come and read Rossetti here
    by a Japanese-y lamp

158. Sketches at a fancy dress ball in the Bedford Park Club.

159. The corner of Bedford Road and Queen Anne's Grove. The house on the right was designed by R. Norman Shaw; the house on the left by E.W. Godwin. Drawing by T.A. Greeves.

While 'Arry' shouts to 'Hemmua':
     'Say ere's a bloomin lark,
Them's the biled lobster 'ouses
     as folks call Bedford Park."

G.K.Chesterton parodied Bedford Park as Saffron Park in *The Man who was Thursday*. The exotically-dressed inhabitants are described as being themselves 'a work of art who made the real thing superfluous...' and it was 'an artistic colony though it never in any definable way produced any art'. This is rather unfair since many well known artists, illustrators, craftspeople, writers, actors and architects lived in Bedford Park. It also attracted army officers, lawyers, clergymen and doctors.

There are two other houses of particular architectural interest in Bedford Park: 14 South Parade, an 'artist's cottage' designed by C.F.A. Voysey in 1891, faced in roughcast, perhaps in deliberate defiance of its red-brick neighbours, and 2 South Parade, a product of the Bauhaus school, built on the site of a Norman Shaw house in 1938 by Dugdale and Ruhemann.

160. The interior of the Bedford Park Club, showing the Ladies' Drawing Room

The War Years

WORLD WAR I

The fabric of Chiswick was relatively unscathed during the First World War, although inevitably residents suffered many privations. From the outset, people played their part in housing the many Belgian refugees fleeing from the invading Germans and matinees were held at the Chiswick Empire to raise money for the Chiswick War Fund.

There was a rush to enlist at Chiswick Town Hall, following Kitchener's 'your country needs you' recruiting drive in 1915. After conscription was introduced in 1916, the Chiswick Empire was raided during an evening performance by military police checking the credentials of all males between 18-41.

As the German U-Boat blockade tightened its grip on the country, food became scarce. The Council made more land available for allotments and Chiswick residents were urged to breed rabbits to eke out the meat supply. Emergency Food Depots were opened at the National Schools, Turnham Green and the parish rooms of St Mary Magdalene in Bennett Street, St James, Gunnersbury and St Michael and All

Angels, Bedford Park in 1918 – the year that rationing was introduced.

Local firms went over to war work and the lake at Grove House was commandeered for building concrete barges to take ammunition to France. Material for munitions became scarce and local children with all kinds of implements – chisels, hammers, bodkins and nails – were sent out to dig up whatever pieces of metal they could find in the wooden pavements.

In 1915 the Council had offered to deliver sand to all ratepayers to put out incendiary bombs. However, it wasn't needed until the war was almost over. An air raid came close to Chiswick in 1917 and a missile fell through the roof of Our Lady of Grace, Duke's Avenue, embedding itself in the floor and knocking off the wheels of a pram. Luckily the missile didn't explode.

Zeppelins were also seen over Chiswick in 1917. One, hit by anti-aircraft guns, caught fire: 'the blazing mass, in the midst of which the ribs could be plainly seen, took a dip downwards and slowly, very slowly, came to earth'.

In January 1918, Chiswick took a direct hit when 14 bombs fell in Isleworth, Brentford and Chiswick within six minutes. Three bombs fell on Chiswick High Road, injuring five people, smashing the gas and

161. In 1920 this tank, which had served in France, was given to Chiswick in recognition of money raised for the war effort, and was set up on the western end of Turnham Green. Many Chiswick residents didn't appreciate the gesture: 'it came to Chiswick unheralded, let it depart unwept', wrote one correspondent to the local paper. The tank was dismantled and sold for scrap in 1937.

BOROUGH OF B——D AND C——K

WARNING!

to all Shopkeepers, Householders and Others

A

PUBLIC TEAR GAS TEST

will be held on a day during the
Week of 3rd—8th NOVEMBER, 1941

THE WARNING will be given by the SOUNDING
of RATTLES.

IMMEDIATELY such warning is sounded the following steps MUST
be taken;—

1. All exposed foods must be sufficiently protected.

   (a) Put food in refrigerators, or
   (b) Cover with grease-proof paper.

2. All doors and windows Must be closed.

3. All Persons inside the premises must PUT ON
   THEIR GAS MASKS at ONCE and keep
   them in position until the " ALL CLEAR OF
   GAS " is sounded.

4. All Ventilating Plant must be shut off.

5. Once Doors and Windows are closed, NO ONE
   must be allowed to ENTER or LEAVE the
   Premises.

*162. In the early years of World War II, it was feared that
poison gas would be dropped on Britain, so everyone was
issued with a gas mask, and gas drills, like the one advertised
here, were held.*

*163. This concrete pill box on the railway line at Strand-on-
the-Green (beside the bridge over the road) is one of several
that still remain on the railway lines in Chiswick. Pill boxes
were strung out in lines across the countryside – a sort of
twentieth-century Hadrian's Wall – as part of Britain's early
defence strategy against possible invasion.*

WORLD WAR II

'Keep calm and carry on' was the headline in the local
paper, following the radio announcement at 11.15 am
on Sunday, 3 September 1939 that Britain was at war
with Germany. This time Britain was prepared: ARP
(Air Raid Precautions) posts were already in place;
conscription and rationing were introduced quickly
and a blackout imposed, which inevitably led to a
huge increase in the number of crimes and road
accidents in Chiswick.

SHELTERS

As protection against air raids, Anderson shelters,
distributed free to the less wealthy, were sunk into
gardens. They came in galvanised steel sections for
assembly and were 6ft high, 6ft long and 4ft 6" wide.
In 1941, indoor, Morrison shelters (6ft by 6ft and 2ft 9"
high) were introduced. It must have been a tight
squeeze for the two adults, one older child and two
younger children supposed to fit inside them.

Trenches for public air raid shelters were dug on
Turnham Green, Stamford Brook Common, Back
Common, in the Gunnersbury Triangle, the grounds
of Chiswick House, at Strand-on-the-Green and the
sewage works in Pumping Station Road.

Basements were commandeered for underground
shelters, the largest being that in Devonshire Works,
Duke's Avenue which had room for 877. Other public
shelters were the Griffin Brewery, the Congrega-
tional Church in Chiswick High Road, 46-48 Turnham
Green Terrace, 1-3 Chiswick Lane, 15 Grove Park
Terrace, 55 Grove Park Gardens, 5, 7, 9 and 109 Grove
Park Road, 60, 144, 146, 152 Sutton Court Road, 41

water mains, and damaging surrounding property.

The day war ended in 1918, the church bells pealed,
the flags were raised and people danced in the streets,
despite the pouring rain, and in July 1919 Chiswick
was *en fête*, holding what was described as 'the biggest peace fair in history', along with a thanksgiving
service, a processional pageant, games, concerts and
theatres. 'The manner in which Chiswick celebrated
peace should pass down in history as one of the
town's finest achievements' said the local paper.

The Council discussed how best to commemorate
the dead. Rejecting the suggestion of a sunken bandstand on Turnham Green, the Council decided to
build more almshouses – the War Memorial Homes of
Rest off Burlington Lane – and to put up a memorial
arch on Turnham Green inscribed with the names of
the fallen, designed by Maurice B. Adams.

However, public subscriptions for this dried up
and the present, more modest, memorial was erected
instead. Bedford Park put up its own war memorial –
the seat opposite the hall of St Michael and All Angels.

Oxford Road. Later in the war, brick surface shelters were built.

The inadequacy of the shelters became apparent during the Blitz. They were cold and damp and the Griffin Brewery shelter flooded. Sanitary conditions were poor. The mayor of Brentford and Chiswick described them as 'nauseous and too appalling for words' and they were inevitably a breeding ground for infections: 'sleeping head to toe is advised' said a pamphlet put out by the Central Council for Health Education, 'because if a neighbour sneezes, your toes, being opposite his head, can take it'.

EVACUATION

An evacuation of children from London and other cities began at the outset of the war. Chiswick children were marched to the Town Hall, clutching their gas masks and clothes in a case or bundle. There they boarded buses to unknown destinations – many went to Hertfordshire, Buckinghamshire and Cornwall.

Evacuation was, however, not compulsory and in November 1940 the local paper was complaining that there were still too many children in Chiswick. Pleas of poverty or fears that children might be unhappy were the reasons for non-evacuation advanced by parents. The schools, which had closed at the beginning of the war, reopened later with air raid shelters provided (three bombs landed on Chiswick County School in Burlington Lane).

FOOD

More land in Chiswick was allocated for allotments as a result of the Government's 'dig for victory' campaign, and the local paper contained regular tips on what to grow and how. Food rationing began in January 1940. The weekly ration was pretty meagre (only 8oz of meat a week). Clothes, soap and coal were rationed later.

Worried that people might not be eating adequately, the Government recommended the setting up of community restaurants. A 'British Restaurant' opened in August 1941 at the Catholic Church Hall in Chiswick Common Road. It served a three-course midday meal plus tea or coffee for 1/2d (6p in today's money).

FUNDING THE WAR EFFORT

Chiswick gave generously to the fund for war weapons. Per head of population, Chiswick contributed more money than any other Middlesex borough in War Weapons Week, May 1941. The money went to build tanks, ships, Lancaster bombers and a spitfire bearing the Borough's name. Sadly, the 'Borough of Brentford and Chiswick' spitfire only clocked up 60 flying hours. On 9 May 1942 it failed to return while on operations over France.

THE BOMBING

In a determined effort to break the British spirit, the

164. Raising money for the war effort. As part of Warship Week, March 1941, a large model of HMS Opportune was built on Turnham Green (see Ill. 165). The Mayor and Mayoress are on board along with members of the Chiswick Rescue Squad responsible for building the model.

165. The model warship, HMS Opportune, *on Turnham Green in March 1941.*

Germans began the heavy night-time bombing of London – the Blitzkrieg (lightning strike) – on 7 September 1940. The first bombs to land on Chiswick fell at 11.30pm in the Burlington Lane, Chiswick Mall, Hogarth Lane areas. These were incendiary bombs which burnt out without causing much damage. Bombs of various types fell every night, bar three, for the rest of the month, and continued to fall, with brief respites, until May 1941.

The first fatality was caused by a bomb in Belmont Road, Turnham Green on 16 September. Three people were killed the following day in Staveley Road. Other bombing incidents that caused death or severe damage were: at Strand-on-the-Green on 21 September when a parachute mine landed, destroying 41 houses in Thames Road and Magnolia Road and severely damaging 60 more. On 28 September there was a major fire when the Army and Navy Furniture Depository was hit, and on the same night, a bomb in Hogarth Lane killed seven people and damaged many properties, including Hogarth House.

On 10 October, six people were killed in Oxford Road and a bomb in Blandford Road on the 20th demolished two houses and damaged many others in Blandford Road, Fielding Road, Marlborough Crescent and the Avenue. Three people were killed outright on 10 November in Riverview Grove when their Anderson shelter was blown out of the ground.

No bombs fell on Chiswick during 1942 or 1943, so the 'baby blitz' of early 1944 came as something of a surprise. Particularly disruptive was the bomb that fell at the junction of Chiswick High Road and Duke's Avenue on 19 February, which fractured water, gas and electricity mains, broke the telephone and trolley bus wires, badly damaged the Roman Catholic Church and killed three people. Bombs on 23 February killed five people in Wolseley Gardens and three in Barrowgate Road. The following day several bombs in the Acton area of Chiswick caused more casualties and extensive damage to houses.

FLYING BOMBS

In 1944 Germany began to bombard Britain with a new kind of weapon: the flying bomb (doodle-bug). Known as the V1 (which stands for *Vergeltungswaffe Eins* – 'revenge weapon one') these 'pilotless planes' were launched from ground ramps or from aircraft and carried a tonne of explosive. The first doodle-bug in Chiswick arrived on 18 June when Cubitts Yacht Basin took a direct hit – six boats were sunk and one person killed. Flying bombs also caused fatalities and damage in Thornton Avenue, Homefield Road and Fletcher Road before the allies were able to overrun the launch sites.

In early September 1944 people were becoming

more relaxed; there had been no alerts for several days and the papers of 7 September carried a cheerful speech from Home Secretary, Herbert Morrison, proclaiming that Germany had lost the battle of London. The very next day Hitler launched his most insidious weapon yet – the V2 rocket. The first landed, totally without warning, on Chiswick.

It was 6.34pm on a drizzly Friday evening when there was a loud explosion and a huge crater, 40ft across, 20ft deep, appeared in the middle of Staveley Road, a development of middle class housing put up in the 1920s. The rocket landed opposite No 5, which had to be demolished along with ten other houses. Fifteen more needed extensive rebuilding and 658 others were damaged.

Sapper Bernard Robert Browning, walking along the road to see his girlfriend, was killed, as was three year-old Rosemary Clarke asleep in her cot, and 65-year-old housewife, Mrs Harrison, sitting by the kitchen fire. Twenty-four other people were injured.

Because of its speed, radar was unable to detect the V2 and people had no chance to take cover since its approach could be neither seen nor heard. It just zoomed out of the sky emitting a tremendous bang as the war head exploded, followed by a long drawn out rumbling.

The V2 explosion in Staveley Road was heard as far away as Westminster, where those in the know recognised that something new and sinister was afoot.

Within an hour, Staveley Road was full of VIPs, including Herbert Morrison himself. In an attempt to mislead the Germans, news of the V2's arrival was suppressed, people were told that a gas main had exploded (the local paper forbore to report *any* incident in Staveley Road the following week).

After 25 more V2s landed in areas around London during the next ten days the gas explosion explanation began to wear a bit thin – 'another Chiswick gas main' became a standard joke for any loud bang – but it wasn't until November that the people were told about the rocket.

In the area defined as Chiswick in this book, there were about 440 'incidents', the term given to reports of high explosive bombs, parachute mines, phosphorous bombs, flying bombs, rockets, AA shells and clusters of incendiaries. In the Hounslow part of Chiswick, 52 people died and many more were injured. Casualties for the Acton section of Chiswick are not available.

When victory in Europe was announced in May 1945, bonfires were lit and the streets were festooned with flags. Many pubs ran out of drink and didn't open the following day. In July 1945, former Chiswick resident, Field Marshal Montgomery, received the freedom of the Borough of Brentford and Chiswick at the Chiswick Empire after a procession along the High Road from Young's Corner. When Japan surrendered in August 1945, the war finally came to an end.

166. The devastation caused by the bomb which fell at the junction of Duke's Avenue and the High Road on 19 February 1944. The building in the background is North Lodge, depot of Express Dairy (it has been replaced by the Catholic Centre).

167. *Air raid damage in Fishers Lane, September 1940.*

168. *Home Secretary, Herbert Morrison and other officials inspecting the crater in Staveley Road on 9 September 1944, the day after the first V2 rocket landed. The houses have now been rebuilt to their original designs and new flowering cherry trees (for which Staveley Road is famous) planted.*

169. *This little shop at 6 Burlington Lane was demolished to make way for the Hogarth roundabout. Archaeologists found a large amount of pottery dating from the 17th and 18th centuries beneath it.*

Shops and Offices

Stalls pitched in the street, and the front rooms of houses served as shops in early centuries. The merchandise included produce from Brentford, where there had been a market since 1306, and commodities brought in by itinerant street traders, as well as local goods.

A commercial directory of 1826-7 lists 40 shops in Chiswick, including eleven grocers and cheesemongers, nine bakers, seven butchers, five boot and shoe makers, two linen drapers, a saddler and a toy shop. As the population increased, so did the number of shops, especially in Chiswick High Road, where, at the end of the century, they were described as being 'particularly good'. Away from the High Road, there were shops in Old Chiswick, Strand-on-the-Green and Stamford Brook.

Some of the better known, or longer lived shops are described below.

OLD SHOPS

Young's Corner, which marks the boundary of Chiswick and Hammersmith, takes its name from a grocery store and post office run by several generations of a family called Young at the junction of King Street and Goldhawk Road. Charles Spencer Young, the last owner of the shop, was an antiquarian as well as a grocer and displayed his collection of satirical political prints in the shop window for the amusement of customers. The corner was rebuilt in 1894 when the area was redeveloped, but the Young name is immortalised in a plaque on the Victorian building now on the site.

Meat was brought to Chiswick 'on the hoof'. Chiswick had seven slaughterhouses in 1891, one of them belonging to Caught's the butcher, which traded from a site opposite Turnham Green Common from at least 1852 to 1959 – these premises were demolished to make way for a Waitrose supermarket, now Iceland.

170. *Young's Corner in 1880. Young's grocery shop is on the right. The building on the left was a farm with thirteen acres of market gardens stretching north beyond it.*

171. *Caught's the butcher traded from 396 Chiswick High Road (opposite Turnham Green) for over seventy years.*

The shop Chiswick residents miss most is Goodban's department store at 326-332 Chiswick High Road. Goodban's was a general store with thirty departments where 'everything from a packet of pins to a carpet could be bought'. Percy Goodban took over what was already an established drapery business from William Soper in 1909. Soper had opened in 1893 and advertisements claimed his shop as 'the largest draper, milliner and mantle warehouse and leading fashion emporium in the neighbourhood'.

Goodban's closed in 1974. There were plans to demolish the building and replace it with another department store, but nothing came of these, and in 1977 a branch of Boots and a branch of Cato (now Robert Dyas) moved into the premises.

Goodban's, however, was not Chiswick's oldest drapery store. This was Rankin's which opened in 1858 as a tiny corner shop on the junction of Chiswick High Road and Windmill Place; it expanded and traded for 110 years before being sold to Salem Carpets in 1968 (a new building has gone up on the site and Endsleigh Insurance occupy the original Rankin's shop).

Durbin and Allwright was a high class provisions merchant in Turnham Green Terrace. It opened in 1900 as two shops – a grocer and a poultry shop – and was apparently a great place for swapping gossip. It contracted to one shop, famous for its marvellous cheeses, and closed in the 1980s.

In 1926 there was an indoor market on the corner of Linden Gardens and the High Road. It was designed to take market stalls off the street, where they had become an eyesore. Accommodating 47 stalls, it was initially very successful but trade gradually dwindled. When the market closed in 1936 the building was adapted for the fire service (the police station was built on the site in 1972).

EXISTING SHOPS

A 'penny bazaar' was opened in Marks and Spencer's present premises in 1910. In those days it was a long narrow shop with a counter running down one side. Boots had branches in Chiswick High Road (Nos. 28 and 282) by 1903; Woolworth's by 1921. Cullens in Chiswick High Road is a successor to an earlier Cullens which, from 1913, was on the western corner of Turnham Green Terrace and Chiswick High Road until it closed in the 1960s. Service, rather than convenience, was Cullens' selling platform in those days: not only did it deliver (as indeed did most shops) but it would also send someone round to collect your order, so saving you the bother of going to the shop at all. Sainsbury's massive supermarket opened in 1986 and this led to the demise of Chiswick's former large supermarket, Waitrose in 1987.

172. Waiting for the doors to open at Goodban's sale in 1909. Note the name of the previous shop, William Soper, still on the front.

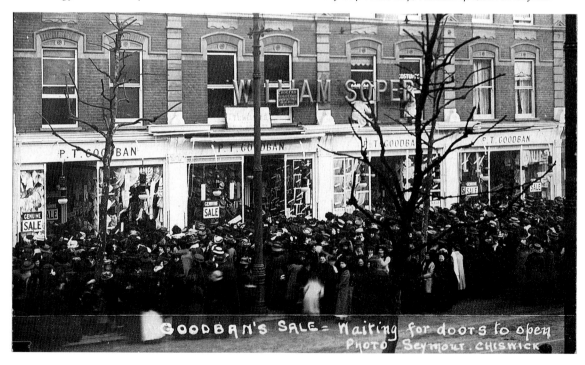

OFFICES

Given the proximity of the Great West Road and its 'golden mile' of factory and office development, Chiswick has perhaps been lucky to have escaped excessive commercialisation and industrialisation. The pockets of non-residential development largely cluster around the west end of the High Road, Hogarth roundabout and Edensor Road with other piecemeal developments elsewhere.

The first office tower blocks were put up in the 1960s, the earliest, the eleven-storey building, Empire House (414 Chiswick High Road), which replaced the Chiswick Empire, in 1961. At the time this was welcomed as a 'most desirable building, especially as most of the area along Chiswick High Road is architecturally nondescript'.

The largest office building is the L-shaped 18-storey block built over Gunnersbury station between 1964-1966. Staff and visitors can enter the building directly from the station. Designed to accommodate 1,500 people, it was the headquarters of IBM between 1966-1992. After extensive alterations, it became the home of the British Standards Institution in 1994.

174. Mylo's, famous for its ice cream and its 1930s facade, was at 253 Chiswick High Road from 1938 to 1983.

173. Delivery boys outside the premises of F.H. Hubbard, baker and post office, in the Avenue, Bedford Park.

F. H. HUBBARD, *Bread and Biscuit Baker,*

PASTRYCOOK

AND

CONFECTIONER.

Awarded 5 Gold and Silver Medals and Diplomas of Merit for Best Bread, 1900, 1901 and 1902.

———※———

Noted for our Celebrated Pure Home-made Bread.
School, Sponge, Madeira, Wedding and Birthday Cakes.
Ices, etc.
Breakfast, Dinner and Milk Rolls.
Self-Raising Flour.

All Orders punctually attended to.   Families waited on.
Special Terms for Schools, Parties, etc.

———※———

POST   OFFICE.

The Avenue Bakery, Bedford Park, W.

ALSO AT 159, ACTON LANE.

Current policy, as outlined in the Chiswick Local Plan of 1988, doesn't favour more high-rise building. The area south of Chiswick High Road, together with Bedford Park is described as being 'sensitive to the impact of high buildings' and 'proposals to erect high buildings will normally be unacceptable' (although various exceptions to this are listed).

BARLEY MOW WORKSPACE

In 1974 the old Sanderson factory in Barley Mow Passage became the Barley Mow Workspace. Workspaces are alternatives to offices for new businesses or small firms which need an administrative base but don't want to be crippled with expensive overheads. The workspace rents out small office or industrial units and lays on services and facilities, the costs of which are shared by the occupants.

The Barley Mow Workspace grew out of a much smaller workspace in Covent Garden and was one of the first planned workspaces in Britain.

POSTSCRIPT

Today Chiswick may be just another London suburb, but it is a distinguished one: not only does it retain many traces of its existence as four rural villages but what survives is of high quality, both aesthetically and historically. How secure, though, is Chiswick's heritage?

Five separate parts of the area defined as Chiswick in this book are designated conservation areas – Bedford Park, Chiswick House area, Old Chiswick, Strand-on-the-Green and Turnham Green – and over 450 houses and other buildings are listed by English Heritage. What's more, Chiswick residents care about their environment and have mounted many successful campaigns to protect it. They, for instance, prevented Hounslow Council closing Hogarth House and thwarted a plan to develop the Gunnersbury Triangle. This is now a nature reserve.

There are several well-established and active local societies: the Brentford and Chiswick Local History Society, Bedford Park Society, Chiswick House Area Residents Association, Old Chiswick Protection Society, Strand-on-the-Green Association, Grove Park Group, East Chiswick Residents Association and the Mid-Chiswick Society.

All these factors should guarantee some degree of protection for Chiswick's historical identity, and, if the Chiswick Local Plan (supplemented by the London Borough of Hounslow's Unitary Development Plan) is adhered to, new non-residential development will be confined to the already-industrialised

175. *Shopping in Chiswick market, 1925, now the site of the police station.*

parts of Chiswick, and the style of the building be 'sympathetic to the area'. The worry is how this will be interpreted – the undecided future of the old London Transport bus works opposite Gunnersbury Park Station, for instance, with its proposed 1.5m sq. feet of office accommodation and parking for 3,000 cars, could strain Chiswick's roads and resources and affect its character.

Those of us who care about Chiswick's heritage must be vigilant to safeguard it, and so prevent the faceless expansion that has swallowed up so many areas of outer London.

175. *(Top right) Empire House, 414 Chiswick High Road, built on the site of the Chiswick Empire in 1961. It was reclad in reflective plate glass in 1983.*

176. *The office block built over Gunnersbury station 1964-66. Formerly the headquarters of IBM, it is now the home of the British Standards Institution.*

Further Reading

Arthure, Humphrey: *Life and Work in Old Chiswick* Old Chiswick Protection Society, 1982.

Arthure, Humphrey: *Thornycroft's Shipbuilding and Motor Works in Chiswick.*

Bolsterli, Margaret: *The Early Community at Bedford Park* 1977.

Bowack, John: *Antiquities of Middlesex* 1705-6 (the section on Chiswick parish is contained in Phillimore & Whitear - see below).

Brentford and Chiswick Local History Society: *Journal* (vol 1, 1980; vol 2, 1981; vol 3, 1982; vol 4, 1985).

Coleman, Reginald & Seaton, Shirley: *Stamford Brook, an Affectionate Portrait* 1992.

Draper, Warwick: *Chiswick* 1973 (first published 1923).

Duttson, Lawrence: *Mainly about Bedford Park People* 1994.

Faulkner, Thomas: *The History and Antiquities of Brentford, Ealing and Chiswick* 1845.

Gilbert, Mizpah: *Chiswick Old and New* 1932.

Green, Florence M: *Hogarth and His House* 1988.

Greeves, T. Affleck: *Bedford Park* (articles reproduced from *Country Life*, 1967)

Greeves, T. Affleck: *Bedford Park, the First Garden Suburb* 1975.

Greeves, T. Affleck: *Guide to Bedford Park 'the first Garden Suburb' in the form of Two Walks* Bedford Park Society, 1983.

Hammond, Carolyn: *Chiswick Library: 100 years of service to the community* 1991.

Hammond, Carolyn & Peter: *Chiswick* 1994.

Hounslow, London Borough of: *Brentford and Chiswick as it Was, a selection of Victorian and Edwardian photographs* compiled and annotated by Brentford and Chiswick Local History Society and Hounslow Library Services 1978.

Hounslow, London Borough of: *Chiswick as it Was, a selection of Victorian and early 20th century photographs* compiled and annotated by London Borough of Hounslow, Department of Arts and Recreation and the Brentford and Chiswick Local History Society, 1986

Lysons, Daniel: *Environs of London* 1810 (the section on the history of Chiswick is contained in Phillimore & Whitear - see below).

Pearce, Sybil: *An Edwardian Childhood in Bedford Park (1900-1910)* 1977.

Pearce, Sybil: *The Years Between: Remiscences of Bedford Park Between the Wars (1919-39)* 1990.

Pearce, Sybil: *A Post Edwardian Girlhood in Bedford Park* 1983.

Phillimore W.P.W. & Whitear, W.H. (eds): *Historical Collections relating to Chiswick* 1897.

Reed, Nicholas: *Pisarro in West London.*

Roe, William P: *Glimpses of Chiswick's Place in History* 1990.

Sanders, Lloyd: *Old Kew, Chiswick and Kensington* 1910

Shaw, Christine: *The Rebuilding of Chiswick Vicarage 1657-8.*

Victoria History of the Counties of England volume VII: *A History of Middlesex* 1982.

Wisdom, James & Bott, Valerie: *A Walk Round the Grove Park Estate, Chiswick* The Grove Park Group & the Brentford & Chiswick Local History Society, 1980

178. *The conservatory and palm house belonging to Fromow's nursery, built in the 1890s on the corner of Sutton Lane and Wellesley Road.*

INDEX
Illustrations are indicated by an asterisk